DISCARD

Pocket
HAVANA
TOP SIGHTS • LOCAL LIFE • MADE EASY

Brendan Sainsbury

In This Book

QuickStart Guide

Your keys to understanding the city – we help you decide what to do and how to do it

Need to Know
Tips for a smooth trip

Neighborhoods
What's where

Explore Havana

The best things to see and do, neighborhood by neighborhood

Top Sights
Make the most of your visit

Local Life
The insider's city

The Best of Havana

The city's highlights in handy lists to help you plan

Best Walks
See the city on foot

Havana's Best...
The best experiences

Survival Guide

Tips and tricks for a seamless, hassle-free city experience

Arriving in Havana
Travel like a local

Essential Information
Including where to stay

Our selection of the city's best places to eat, drink and experience:

- ◉ Sights
- ✖ Eating
- ⭕ Drinking
- ✪ Entertainment
- 🔒 Shopping

These symbols give you the vital information for each listing:

- ☎ Telephone Numbers
- ◷ Opening Hours
- P Parking
- Ⓝ Nonsmoking
- @ Internet Access
- 📶 Wi-Fi Access
- ✔ Vegetarian Selection
- 📖 English-Language Menu
- 👪 Family-Friendly
- 🐾 Pet-Friendly
- 🚌 Bus
- ⛴ Ferry
- Ⓜ Metro
- Ⓢ Subway
- 🚋 Tram
- 🚆 Train

Find each listing quickly on maps for each neighborhood:

Bar Hemingway

16 ⭕ Map p233, B2

Legend has it that Hemi self, wielding a machine rate this timber-pan ered bar during showpiece is a en by Papa ar town. Dress s.com; Hôtel Rit ⊙6.30pm-2a

Lonely Planet's Havana

Lonely Planet Pocket Guides are designed to get you straight to the heart of the city.

Inside you'll find all the must-see sights, plus tips to make your visit to each one really memorable. We've split the city into easy-to-navigate neighborhoods and provided clear maps so you'll find your way around with ease. Our expert authors have searched out the best of the city: walks, food, nightlife and shopping, to name a few. Because you want to explore, our 'Local Life' pages will take you to some of the most exciting areas to experience the real Havana.

And of course you'll find all the practical tips you need for a smooth trip: itineraries for short visits, how to get around, and how much to tip the guy who serves you a drink at the end of a long day's exploration.

It's your guarantee of a really great experience.

Our Promise

You can trust our travel information because Lonely Planet authors visit the places we write about, each and every edition. We never accept freebies for positive coverage, so you can rely on us to tell it like it is.

The Best of Havana | 121

Havana's Best Walks

Havana's Best ...

Survival Guide | 143

QuickStart Guide

Welcome to Havana

On first impressions, Havana can seem like a confusing jigsaw puzzle, but work out how to put the pieces together and a beautiful picture emerges. It's too audacious, too contradictory, and, despite 60 years of withering neglect, too damn beautiful. How it does it is anyone's guess. Maybe it's the swashbuckling history, the survivalist spirit, or the indefatigable salsa energy that emanates most emphatically from the people. Arrive with an open mind and prepare for a long, slow seduction.

Salsa in Havana
LESINKA372/SHUTTERSTOCK ©

Havana
Top Sights

Museo Nacional de Bellas Artes (p50)

Cuba's finest art gallery.

DIEGO GRANDI/SHUTTERSTOCK ©

Parque Histórico Militar Morro-Cabaña (p26)

Unmissable military park.

Plaza Vieja (p28)

Havana's most eclectic colonial square.

Museo de la Revolución (p52)

Cuban history housed in one of Havana's finest palaces.

Catedral de la Habana (p30)

The pinnacle of Cuban baroque architecture.

Fusterlandia (p88)

Mosaic art on steroids.

Museo Hemingway (p118)

Museum honoring America's greatest Cuba-phile.

Necrópolis Cristóbal Colón (p68)

Finest cemetery in the Americas.

Iglesia de Nuestra Señora de Regla (p108)

Church immersed in legend.

Havana
Local Life

*Local experiences and hidden gems
to help you uncover the real city*

Havana is a visceral place. The best sights can't be located on any map. To find them you'll need patience, spontaneity and a sturdy pair of legs. Walk the streets and investigate.

Centro Habana Streetlife (p54)
☑ Shopping streets ☑ People-watching

MIAMI2YOU/SHUTTERSTOCK ©

Rehabilitated Habana Vieja (p32)
☑ Colonial architecture ☑ Social projects

Vedado by Night (p70)
☑ Live music ☑ Dancing

JAMES HACKLAND/ALAMY ©

Guanabacoa (p110)
☑Historic buildings ☑Old churches

FELIX LIPOV/ALAMY ©

Unsignposted Playa (p90)
☑Arty cafes ☑Leafy pathways

Other great places to experience the city like a local:

Plaza del Cristo (p38)

Los Nardos (p62)

Plaza de Armas Secondhand Book Market (p47)

Cojímar (p103)

Convento & Iglesia del Carmen (p60)

Cuba Libro (p85)

Don Cangrejo (p95)

LGBT Vedado (p80)

Regla Streetlife (p117)

Calle Obispo (p39)

AHOWDEN INTERNATIONAL/ALAMY ©

Havana's Eastern Beaches (p100)
☑ Sandy beaches ☑ Water sports

Havana
Day Planner

Day One

Explore Habana Vieja by strolling the streets between the four main colonial squares, stopping for morning coffee in **Plaza Vieja** (p28) and browsing through the revolutionary tomes at the secondhand book market in **Plaza de Armas** (p41). Soak up the atmosphere on shop- and museum-lined **Calle Mercaderes** (p33) before making a beeline for baroque **Catedral de la Habana** (p30).

Get your introduction to Havana's layered art culture by visiting the 'Arte Cubano' collection of the **Museo Nacional de Bellas Artes** (p50). Afterwards, walk down the wide avenue El Prado and turn left into the **Malecón** (p55) sea drive – aka Havana's outdoor living room – in time for sunset.

For Havana's trendiest after-dark quarter, gravitate to **Plaza del Cristo** (p38), where live music pulsates in cool bars and events are sometimes organized outside in the square.

Day Two

Start the morning with coffee and/or breakfast in the pleasant square in front of **Café del Ángel Fumero Jacqueline** (p42). It's a short hop from here to **Museo de la Revolución** (p52) encased in the impossible-to-miss Presidential Palace. When you've had your fill of revolutionary propaganda, proceed to **Parque Central** (p59) where you can catch the Habana Bus Tour to Vedado.

Recline beneath the pillars of wisdom in the **Universidad de la Habana** (p74). before visiting its two on-site museums. You'll probably want to reserve more time for the excellent **Museo Napoleónico** (p74) across the street. Afterwards, wander over to the **Coppelia** (p70) for a low-cost Cuban-style ice cream.

Have a mojito on the outdoor terrace at the **Hotel Nacional** (p74) and find out if there are tickets for **Cabaret Parisien** (p83). Book, or pay at the door, and get ready to enjoy one of Havana's best nights out.

Short on time?
We've arranged Havana's must-sees into these day-by-day itineraries to make sure you see the very best of the city in the time you have available.

Day Three

☀ Hang out around **Parque Central** (p59) admiring the old American cars in front of the Capitolio Nacional and the lobbies of some of the historic hotels nearby. Brush up on the Santería religion in the **Asociación Cultural Yoruba de Cuba** (p59) and take a guided tour around the recently restored **Gran Teatro de la Habana Alicia Alonso** (p63).

☀ Get a bus or taxi to take you to San Francisco de Paula to visit the **Museo Hemingway** (p119). Factor in an hour to see the museum and an hour for the return journey (longer for the bus). On the way back, continue the Hemingway theme by squeezing into **La Bodeguita del Medio** (p45) for an obligatory mojito.

☾ Head over to the **Fortaleza de San Carlos de la Cabaña** (p27) for the famous cañonazo ceremony at 9pm. Be sure to arrive before 8pm to allow time to look around the fort and its museums and admire the nighttime views of Havana. Afterwards, return to Habana Vieja and wander the atmospheric streets until you find a musical bar to draw you in.

Day Four

☀ Head out to the western end of Playa and visit the amazing community art project known as **Fusterlandia** (p88). On the way back, get a taxi to drop you off on Quinta Avenida. Walk down the broad avenue admiring the eclectic mansions, many of them now embassies.

☀ Cross over the Río Almendares into Vedado, perhaps stopping briefly in the **Parque Almendares** (p90). Head up Calle 23 to Havana's magnificent cemetery, the **Necrópolis Cristóbal Colón** (p68), which is particularly beautiful around 5pm. If there's time, walk over to **Plaza de la Revolución** (p76) to see the Martí Memorial as it's lit up.

☾ Spend the evening at the **Fábrica de Arte Cubano** (p83) – be sure to arrive early (around 8pm) to avoid the crowds. Peruse the art, soak up the atmosphere and check out the night's musical program, all of which should keep you occupied until at least midnight.

Need to Know

**For more information,
see Survival Guide (p143)**

Currency

Cuban convertibles (CUC$) & pesos
(*moneda nacional;* MN$)

Language

Spanish

Visas

Regular tourists require a *tarjeta de turista*
(tourist card) valid for 30 days usually
provided by your flight package. Always
check when booking.

Money

Cuba is primarily a cash economy. Non-US
credit cards are accepted in resort hotels
and some city hotels. There are a growing
number of ATMs.

Mobile Phones

Check with your service provider to see if
your phone will work. You can use your own
GSM or TDMA phones in Cuba, though you'll
have to get a local chip and pay an activation
fee (approximately CUC$30).

Time

Eastern Standard Time (GMT/UTC minus
five hours)

Tipping

Tipping in Cuba is important since most
Cubans earn money in *moneda nacional*
(MN$). Leaving a tip of 10% or more in
convertibles (CUC$) makes a huge difference.

① Before You Go

Your Daily Budget

Budget: Less than CUC$80

▶ Casas particulares: CUC$25–45
▶ Government-run restaurants: CUC$10–15
▶ Cheap museum entry: CUC$1–5

Midrange: CUC$80–170

▶ Midrange hotels: CUC$50–120
▶ Meals in private restaurants: CUC$15–25
▶ Drink in bars: mojito CUC$3

Top End: More than CUC$170

▶ Historic hotel: CUC$200–325
▶ City taxis: CUC$5–10
▶ Evening cabaret: CUC$35–75

Useful Websites

Lahabana.com (www.lahabana.com) Indexed
information on Havana's sights in English,
plus a monthly what's-on guide.

Cuba Casas (www.cubacasas.net) Hugely
comprehensive listings and reviews of
Havana's casas particulares, along with lots
of other useful Cuba information.

Lonely Planet (www.lonelyplanet.com/
havana) Destination information, hotel bookings, traveller forum and more.

Advance Planning

Three months before Check visa require-
ments (especially if you're American), plan a
general itinerary, book flights.

One month before Book hotels and casas
particulares. Check with your bank to see if
your ATM cards will work. Check the tourist
card is included with your flight package.

One week before Reserve Víazul bus
tickets.

② Arriving in Havana

Havana is home to Cuba's main airport, Aeropuerto Internacional José Martí. Since Cuba is an archipelago, almost all foreign visitors (save for cruise passengers) arrive by air. The main bus company is Víazul. Services depart from a terminal 6km from central Havana. Víazul buses run from Havana to practically every city and town in Cuba of interest to tourists.

✈ From José Martí International Airport

A standard taxi to central Havana will cost approximately CUC$20 to CUC$25 (30 to 40 minutes). There is no direct, reliable bus to the city center.

Víazul Bus Terminal

Taxis will charge between CUC$5 and CUC$10 for the 20-minute ride to central Havana. There are no direct metro buses to/from central Havana.

③ Getting Around

Havana is a highly walkable city. Buses and taxis can help bridge the gaps over longer distances.

Bus

A tourist bus called Habana Bus Tour runs on two routes between 9am and 7pm and covers the main tourist sights. Crowded, but cheap metro buses serve more peripheral neighborhoods on 16 different routes.

Taxi

Taxis are ubiquitous, relatively cheap and fill the holes that buses don't reach, especially in outer Havana. Taxis hang around outside all the major tourist hotels, outside the two main bus stations and at various city-center nexus points such as Parque Central and Parque de la Fraternidad. You're never far from a taxi in Havana.

Boat

A regular passenger ferry crosses the harbor between Habana Vieja, Habana del Este, Regla and Guanabacoa.

Havana
Neighborhoods

Vedado (p66)
The modern commercial hub places 1950s skyscrapers alongside wide leafy avenues and a famously buoyant nightlife.

⊙ **Top Sights**
Necrópolis Cristóbal Colón

Habana Vieja (p24)
Thanks to a meticulous restoration program, Havana's original colonial core is crammed with well-preserved historical relics.

⊙ **Top Sights**
Parque Histórico Militar Morro-Cabaña
Plaza Vieja
Catedral de la Habana

Parque Histórico Militar Morro-Cabaña
Museo de la Revolución
Museo Nacional de Bellas Artes
Catedral de la Habana
Plaza Vieja
Iglesia de Nuestra Señora de Regla
Necrópolis Cristóbal Colón

Fusterlandia

Playa & Marianao (p86)
The city's diplomatic quarter is packed with ostentatious mansions, high-end restaurants, convention centers, and a yacht club and marina.

⊙ **Top Sight**
Fusterlandia

Centro Habana (p48)
Havana's most condensed residential district juxtaposes well-maintained museums and hotels with a vibrant grid of mildewed streets.

⊙ **Top Sights**
Museo Nacional de Bellas Artes
Museo de la Revolución

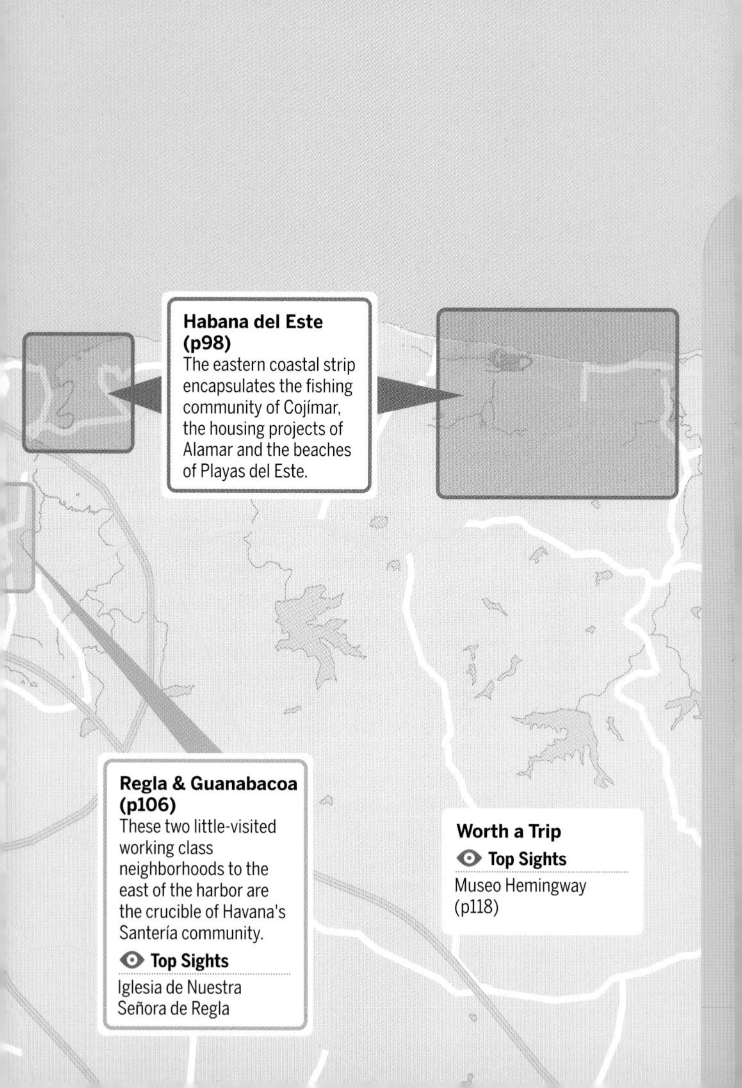

Habana del Este (p98)

The eastern coastal strip encapsulates the fishing community of Cojímar, the housing projects of Alamar and the beaches of Playas del Este.

Regla & Guanabacoa (p106)

These two little-visited working class neighborhoods to the east of the harbor are the crucible of Havana's Santería community.

◉ Top Sights

Iglesia de Nuestra Señora de Regla

Worth a Trip

◉ Top Sights

Museo Hemingway (p118)

Explore
Havana

Worth a Trip

Habana Vieja (p24)
KAMIRA/SHUTTERSTOCK ©

Explore

Habana Vieja

Havana's Old Town is one of the historical highlights of Latin America, an architectural masterpiece where fastidiously preserved squares and grandiose palaces sit alongside a living, breathing urban community still emerging from the economic chaos of the 1990s. The overall result is by turns grand and gritty, inspiring and frustrating, commendable and lamentable. No one should leave Cuba without seeing it.

The Sights in a Day

To tackle history-filled Habana Vieja properly, sit down for breakfast with a map in **La Vitrola** (p42) on the corner of Plaza Vieja, and draw up a strategic plan of attack. The overriding motto: you won't have time to see everything. You can spend a good hour enjoying **Plaza Vieja** (p28) itself before moving onto **Plaza de Armas** (p41) with its **book market** (p47; pictured left) and essential **Museo de la Ciudad** (p36), which will tell you all you need to know about Havana's swashbuckling roots.

Top up your sugar levels in the **Museo del Chocolate** (p44) before strolling down the colonial time capsule of **Calle Mercaderes** (p33). Continue on to the **Catedral de la Habana** (p30) before hailing a cab to take you under the harbor to the **Parque Histórico Militar Morro-Cabaña** (p26). Stay until sunset peacefully perusing the gory details of conflicts past.

Return to the old quarter and go for a long, slow dinner in **El Rum Rum de la Habana** (p39) before hitting the bars and live music scene in **Plaza del Cristo** (p38).

For a local's day in Habana Vieja, see p32.

Top Sights

Parque Histórico Militar Morro-Cabaña (p26)

Plaza Vieja (p28)

Catedral de la Habana (p30)

Local Life

Rehabilitated Habana Vieja (p32)

Best of Havana

Eating

Lamparilla 361 Tapas & Cervezas (p39)

El Rum Rum de la Habana (p39)

Doña Eutimia (p39)

Trattoria 5esquinas (p40)

Donde Lis (p41)

Café del Ángel Fumero Jacqueline (p42)

La Vitrola (p42)

Getting There & Away

Bus The Habana Bus Tour T1 bus stops at various places in Habana Vieja (including Plaza de Armas) before continuing on to Centro Habana, Vedado and Playa.

Ferry Small passenger ferries run from the new Emboque de Luz terminal on Av del Puerto to Casablanca and Regla on the eastern side of Havana's harbor.

Top Sights
Parque Histórico Militar Morro-Cabaña

Making up what was, arguably, the most formidable defensive complex in Spain's erstwhile colonial empire, this unmissable military park, included in the Habana Vieja Unesco World Heritage site, is comprised of two strapping forts: El Morro, with its emblematic lighthouse, and La Cabaña, a sprawling mini-city of a military bastion famed for its sunset-over-the-Malecón views and theatrical cannon-firing ceremony.

Map p34, C1

per fort CUC$6

🕙10am-10pm

Fortaleza de San Carlos de la Cabaña

La Cabaña (Map p34, C2; before/after 6pm CUC$6/8; ⊘10am-10pm) was built between 1763 and 1774 on a long, exposed ridge on the east side of Havana harbor to fill a weakness in the city's defenses. This 18th-century colossus measures 700m from end to end and covers a whopping 10 hectares – it is the biggest Spanish colonial fortress in the Americas. Considered largely impregnable, no invader has ever successfully taken it.

Castillo de los Tres Santos Reyes Magnos del Morro

Perched high on a rocky bluff above the Atlantic, **El Morro** (Map p34, B1; El Morro; CUC$6; ⊘10am-6pm) (the older and smaller of the two forts) was erected between 1589 and 1630 to protect the entrance to Havana harbor from pirates and foreign invaders. The fort's irregular polygonal shape, 3m-thick walls and deep protective moat offer a classic example of Renaissance military architecture. The famous lighthouse was added in 1844.

Cañonazo Ceremony

Every night at 9pm, actors dressed in full 18th-century military regalia reenact the firing of a cannon over the harbor in La Cabaña fort. In days of yore, the shot used to mark the closing of the old city gates. With its solemn marching and the lights of Havana twinkling in the background it's still a highly atmospheric ceremony.

☑ **Top Tips**

▶ Visit at sunset for magnificent views over the city.

▶ If you arrive before 6pm, you'll only have to pay CUC$6 as opposed to the standard CUC$8 evenng rate, but you can still stay to see the *cañonazo* ceremony.

▶ On your walk between the two forts, take time to wander down to the two impressive cannon batteries: Divina Pastora and Doce Apóstoles.

✗ **Take a Break**

There are a couple of bar-restaurants inside La Cabaña fort. For better service and food, head to **Restaurante la Divina Pastora** (Map p34, C2; Parque Histórico Militar Morro-Cabaña; mains CUC$10-18; ⊘noon-11:30pm), a restaurant set in an old building on the harbor shore between the two forts and guarded by a sturdy cannon battery.

Top Sights
Plaza Vieja

Laid out in 1559, Plaza Vieja (Old Square) is Havana's most architecturally eclectic square, where Cuban baroque nestles seamlessly next to Gaudí-inspired art nouveau. Originally called Plaza Nueva (New Square), it was used for military exercises and later served as an open-air marketplace. Unlike Havana's other squares, Plaza Vieja is purely residential and lacks churches, forts or administrative buildings.

Old Square

⊙ Map p34, C6

Palacio Cueto

The distinctive **Palacio Cueto** (cnr Muralla &
Mercaderes), on the southeast corner of the square,
is Havana's finest example of art nouveau. Its
ornate facade, dating from 1906, once fronted a
warehouse and a hat factory before it was rented
by José Cueto in the 1920s as the Palacio Vienna
hotel. Having lain empty since the early 1990s, it
is currently undergoing a seemingly interminable
on-off renovation.

Palacio de los Condes de Jaruco

On the square's southwest corner, **Palacio de los
Condes de Jaruco** (Muralla No 107; admission free;
⊙10am-5pm Mon-Fri, 10am-2pm Sat) was constructed
in 1738 from local limestone in a transitional
mudéjar-baroque style. This muscular mansion is
one of Plaza Vieja's oldest. Rich in period detail,
it is typical of merchant houses of the era. For
many years it was the residence for the exalted
Counts of Jaruco. Today it's the headquarters of
Cuba's main cultural foundation and contains a
small souvenir shop and an art gallery called La
Casona.

The Fountain

A fountain has anchored the square since the
18th century and was originally fashioned in Car-
rara marble by the Italian sculptor, Giorgio Mas-
sari. After being shamefully demolished in the
1950s to make way for an underground car park,
an exact replica of the fountain was installed
in the early 2010s. It was later surrounded by
an elegant black fence, supposedly to stop local
schoolchildren playing in it (the Angela Landa
school abuts the square).

☑ Top Tips

▶ Plaza Vieja is a
decent eating and
drinking option: it
has recently sprouted
some good bars and
restaurants and is one
of Habana Vieja's better
corners for nighttime
action.

▶ Other attractions on
the square worth a look
include a camera obscu-
ra and a plantetarium.

✕ Take a Break

For views of the plaza
action, climb upstairs
to Azúcar Lounge
(p42). For more
intimacy head indoors to
Café Bohemia (p40).

Top Sights
Catedral de la Habana

Havana's incredible cathedral is dominated by two unequal towers and framed by a theatrical baroque facade designed by Italian architect Francesco Borromini. The Jesuits began construction of the church in 1748 and work continued despite their expulsion in 1767. The church was finally consecrated in 1789.

👁 Map p34, C4

cnr San Ignacio & Empedrado

admission free

🕓9am-4:30pm Mon-Fri, 9am-noon Sat & Sun

Front Facade

The cathedral's unusual swirling facade is considered to be the apex of baroque architecture in Cuba. Although visually arresting and unique, the exterior walls were not as lavishly decorated as similar churches in Europe. This is due primarily to the hardness of the local limestone combined with the paucity of skilled craftspeople in 18th-century Cuba. Look closely and you'll see marine fossils embedded in the walls and pillars.

Interior

In contrast to its ornate facade, the cathedral's interior is neoclassical rather than baroque and relatively austere, the result of a puritanical re-modeling by an early-19th-century bishop. There are original Italian frescoes above the altar; the less-valuable oil canvases that adorn the side walls are copies of works by Murillo and Rubens. You can climb the smaller of the cathedral's two towers for CUC$1.

Plaza de la Catedral

The cathedral is ringed by Cuba's most intimate and homogeneous square, a veritable museum to Cuban baroque, with all the surrounding buildings dating from the 1700s. Of particular note is the **Palacio de los Marqueses de Aguas Claras** (San Ignacio No 54) on the west side, a majestic one-time palace completed in 1760 with a beautiful shady Andalucian patio (nowadays it houses the Restaurante Paris). Another beauty is the Palacio de los Condes de Casa Bayona (directly opposite the cathedral), the square's oldest building, dating from 1720, and today occupied by the **Museo de Arte Colonial** (San Ignacio No 61; CUC$2; ⏰9:30am-4:45pm).

☑ Top Tips

▶ Dress appropriately for the church: no sleeveless tops or micro-shorts.

▶ Return to the square at night when it takes on a totally different (and more intimate) atmosphere.

▶ Some of Habana Vieja's best restaurants line a small alley (Callejón del Chorro) just off Plaza de la Catedral.

▶ Listen out for word of live classical music concerts that are sometimes held in the square.

✕ Take a Break

One of the finest exponents of *comida criolla* (traditional Cuban food), Doña Eutimia (p39) is located in a cul-de-sac just off the square's southwest corner along with several other great restaurants. Two blocks from the cathedral, El Rum Rum de la Habana (p39) is one of the city's suavest and most sophisticated restaurants.

Local Life
Rehabilitated Habana Vieja

The piecing together of Habana Vieja began in the late 1970s and is ongoing. The plan, run by the City Historian's Office, has restored Havana's most important historic buildings, created ground-breaking social projects for the local population and garnered numerous international prizes for its cultural, historical and sustainable work.

....

❶ Callejón de los Peluqueros

A small 100m stretch of Calle Aguiar has been transformed into a hairdressing-themed art project by local barber 'Papito' and the City Historian's Office. Anchored by Papito's own salon, which doubles as the Arte Corte museum, **Callejón de los Peluqueros** is augmented by an art studio, a clothes boutique, restaurants and a children's playground.

2 Farmacia Taquechel

Old **Farmacia Taquechel** (📞7-862-9286; Obispo No 155; ⏰9am-6pm) was adapted from an existing townhouse in 1898. Restored in 1996, it functions as both a pharmaceutical museum and a working pharmacy for the local population selling mainly homeopathic medicines.

3 Casa de la Obra Pía

An architectural highlight on Calle Mercaderes is the **Casa de la Obra Pía** (Obrapía No 158; CUC$1.50; ⏰10:30am-5:30pm Tue-Sat, 9:30am-2:30pm Sun), a former Spanish nobleman's mansion. The house was rehabilitated in 1983 as both a museum and community project and now produces textiles made and sold on-site by locals working for a cooperative.

4 Calle Mercaderes

Calle Mercaderes is one of the city's most complete streets and has been undergoing piecemeal restoration since the 1980s. Among its copious businesses are hotels, museums, galleries and shops, but there's also a maternity home, an educational cinema, and a workshop that's revived old manufacturing methods to make artisan paper.

5 Angela Landa School

Plaza Vieja is perhaps the City Historian's most beautifully restored square, but it's not all for tourists. On the north side of the plaza is the **Angela Landa school** that occasionally uses the space as both substitute playground and alfresco classroom. You'll see students running, playing sports, or sitting and reading beneath the giant *portales*.

6 Iglesia y Monasterio de San Francisco de Asís

Originally built in 1608, **Iglesia y Monasterio de San Francisco de Asís** (Oficios, btwn Amargura & Brasil; museum CUC$2; ⏰9am-6pm) ceased to have a religious function in the 1840s. Crypts and religious objects were dug up during excavations in the 1980s, with many of them contained in the Museo de Arte Religioso that opened on the site in 1994. Part of the old monastery is now a children's theater.

7 Iglesia y Convento de Nuestra Señora de Belén

The huge 18th-century **Iglesia y Convento de Nuestra Señora de Belén** (Compostela, btwn Luz & Acosta) was restored by the City Historian in the 1990s, turning the building into an active community center. There are 18 permanent apartments for senior citizens plus a meteorology museum.

E

D

C

B

A

1

2

3

4

Parque Histórico Militar Morro-Cabaña

Castillo de los Tres Santos Reyes Magnos del Morro

Central

Fortaleza de San Carlos de la Cabaña

Restaurante la Divina Pastora

Cañonazo Ceremony

Observatorio Nacional

Estatua de Cristo

CASABLANCA

Casablanca Train Station

Bahía de la Habana

Av Carlos Manuel de Céspedes

Catedral de la Habana

Castillo de la Real Fuerza

Plaza de Armas

Tacón

Callejón del Chorro

Museo de la Ciudad

Obispo

Mstíz

HABANA VIEJA

Centro de Arte Contemporáneo Wifredo Lam

San Ignacio

Parque Maestranza

Cuartel

Tacón

Cuba

Aguiar

Habana

Tejadillo

Chacón

Empedrado

Compostela

Aguacate

Plaza 13 de Marzo

Av de las Misiones

La Casa del Son

Aramonte

Cárcel

Parque de los Enamorados

Parque Mártires del 71

Castillo de San Salvador de la Punta

Malecón

San Lázaro

Paseo de Martí (Prado)

Genios

Refugio

Colón

Trocadero

Ánimas

7

9

20

1

31

12

13

19

22

15

18

17

8

20

Sights

Museo de la Ciudad   MUSEUM

1 ⊙ Map p34, C4

Even with no artifacts, Havana's city museum would be a tour de force, courtesy of the opulent palace in which it resides. Filling the whole west side of Plaza de Armas, the **Palacio de los Capitanes Generales** dates from the 1770s and is a textbook example of Cuban baroque architecture, hewn out of rock from the nearby San Lázaro quarries. A museum has resided here since 1968. (Tacón No 1; CUC$3; ⊙9:30am-6pm)

Castillo de la Real Fuerza   FORT

2 ⊙ Map p34, D4

On the seaward side of Plaza de Armas is one of the oldest existing forts in the Americas, built between 1558 and 1577 on the site of an earlier

fort destroyed by French privateers in 1555. Imposing and indomitable, the castle is ringed by an impressive moat and shelters the **Museo de Navegación**, which covers the history of the fort and Old Town, and its connections with the erstwhile Spanish Empire. Look out for the huge scale model of the *Santíssima Trinidad* galleon. (Plaza de Armas; CUC$3; ⊙9am-5pm Tue-Sun)

Edificio Bacardí   LANDMARK

3 ⊙ Map p34, B5

Finished in 1929, the magnificent Edificio Bacardí is a triumph of art deco architecture with a whole host of lavish finishes that somehow manage to make kitsch look cool. It's hemmed in by other buildings, so it's hard to get a full panoramic view of the structure from street level, though the opulent bell tower can be glimpsed from all over Havana. (Bacardí Bldg; Av de las Misiones, btwn Empedrado & San Juan de Dios; ⊙hours vary)

El Ojo del Ciclón   GALLERY

4 ⊙ Map p34, B5

Just when you think you've seen the strangest, weirdest, surrealist and most avant-garde art, along comes the 'eye of the cyclone' to give you plenty more. The abstract gallery displays the work of Cuban visual artist Leo D'Lázaro and it's pretty mind-bending stuff – giant eyes, crashed cars, painted suitcases and junk reborn as art. Think Jackson Pollock meets

Iglesia y Convento de Nuestra Señora de la Merced

JRR Tolkien at a Psychedelic Furs gig. (📞7-861-5359; O'Reilly No 501, cnr Villegas; admission free; 🕐10am-7pm)

La Casa del Son DANCING, LANGUAGE

5 🎯 Map p34, B4

A highly popular private dance school based in an attractive 18th-century house. It also offers lessons in Spanish language and percussion. Very flexible with class times. (📞7-861-6179; www.bailarencuba.com; Empedrado No 411, btwn Compostela & Aguacate; per hour from CUC$10)

Iglesia y Convento de Nuestra Señora de la Merced CHURCH

6 🎯 Map p34, C7

Bizarrely overlooked by the tourist hordes, this baroque church in its own small square has Havana's most sumptuous ecclesiastical interior, as yet only partially restored. Beautiful gilded altars, frescoed vaults and a number of valuable old paintings create a sacrosanct mood. There's a quiet cloister adjacent. (Cuba No 806; 🕐8am-noon & 3-5:30pm)

Centro de Arte Contemporáneo Wifredo Lam

CULTURAL CENTER

7 ⊙ Map p34, C4

On the corner of Plaza de la Catedral, this cultural center contains the melodious **Cafe Amarillo**, which serves coffee and snacks, and an exhibition center named after the island's most celebrated painter. Rather than displaying Lam's paintings, it hosts some of Havana's best temporary exhibitions of contemporary art. (cnr San Ignacio & Empedrado; CUC$3; ⊙10am-5pm Mon-Sat)

Castillo de San Salvador de la Punta

FORT

8 ⊙ Map p34, A2

One in a quartet of forts defending Havana harbor, La Punta was designed by the Italian military engineer Bautista Antonelli and built between 1589 and 1600. It underwent

Local Life
Plaza del Cristo

In the space of just a few years, Habana Vieja's once overlooked 'fifth' square, **Plaza del Cristo** (Map p34, B6), has become the coolest place to hang out, courtesy of its edgy assortment of bars and shops and occasional live concerts. A little apart from the historical core, it hasn't benefited from a full restoration yet, which is possibly part of its charm.

comprehensive repairs after the British shelled it during their successful 1762 Havana raid. During the colonial era a chain was stretched 250m to the castle of El Morro every night to close the harbor mouth to shipping. (CUC$2; ⊙museum 9:30am-5pm Tue-Sat, 9:30am-noon Sun)

Estatua de Cristo

MONUMENT

9 ⊙ Map p34, E3

This impossible-to-miss statue on a rise on the harbor's eastern side was created by Jilma Madera in 1958. It was promised to President Batista by his wife after the US-backed leader survived an attempt on his life in the Presidential Palace in March 1957, and was (ironically) unveiled on Christmas Day 1958, one week before the dictator fled the country. As you disembark the Casablanca ferry, follow the road uphill for about 10 minutes until you reach the monument.

Museo del Ron

MUSEUM

10 ⊙ Map p34, D6

You don't have to be an Añejo Reserva quaffer to enjoy the Museo del Ron in the Fundación Havana Club, but it probably helps. The museum, with its trilingual guided tour, shows rum-making antiquities and the complex brewing process, but lacks detail or passion. A not overgenerous measure of rum is included in the price. (San Pedro No 262; incl guide CUC$7; ⊙9am-5:30pm Mon-Thu, to 4:30pm Fri-Sun)

Museo-Casa
Natal de José Martí   MUSEUM

11 ◉ Map p34, B8

Opened in 1925, this tiny museum,
set in the house where the apostle
of Cuban independence was born
on January 28, 1853, is considered
to be the oldest in Havana. The City
Historian's Office took the house
over in 1994, and its succinct stash of
exhibits devoted to Cuba's national
hero continues to impress. (Leonor Pérez
No 314; CUC$2; ⊘9:30am-5pm Tue-Sat,
9:30am-1pm Sun)

Eating

Doña Eutimia   CUBAN $$

12 ✕ Map p34, C4

Keep it simple. The secret at Doña
Eutimia is that there is no secret. Just
serve decent-sized portions of incred-
ibly tasty Cuban food. The *ropa vieja*
(shredded beef) and minced beef *pica-
dillo* both deserve a mention. Doña
Eutimia was the first private restaurant to grace this small cul-de-sac
near the cathedral. (Callejón del Chorro
60c; mains CUC$9-12; ⊘noon-10pm)

El Rum Rum
de la Habana   SEAFOOD, SPANISH $$

13 ✕ Map p34, C4

In Cuba, eating establishments are full
of rum (the vital ingredient for mojitos)

◉ Local Life
Calle Obispo

Narrow, chockablock **Calle Obispo**
(Map p34, B5; Bishop's Street), Habana
Vieja's main interconnecting artery,
is packed with art galleries, shops,
music bars and people. Four- and
five-story buildings block out most
of the sunlight, and the swaying
throng of people seems to move in
time to the beautiful din of com-
peting live music that wafts out of
every bar.

and *rum rum* (local term for gossip).
And gossip we must, because El Rum
Rum is the talk of Habana Vieja –
an ambitious new restaurant run by a
cigar sommelier that pays homage to
seafood, Spanish gastronomy, cigars
and throat-warming shots of the
hard stuff. (☎7-861-0806; Empedrado No
256, btwn Cuba & Aguiar; mains CUC$7-13;
⊘noon-midnight)

Lamparilla 361
Tapas & Cervezas   TAPAS $$

14 ✕ Map p34, B5

What makes a new restaurant just...
click? Come to this nascent place on
Lamparilla (never really a happening
street – until now) and try to work
out the secret. Maybe it's the perfect
tapa-sized lasagna, the crisp sautéed
vegetables served in ceramic dishes,
the rich espresso-flavored crème
brûlée, or the table menus written

on dried palm leaves. (📞52-89-53-24; Lamparilla No 361, btwn Aguacate & Villegas; tapas CUC$3-12; ⏱noon-midnight)

Trattoria 5esquinas   ITALIAN $$

15 🍴 Map p34, B4

Best Italian restaurant in Havana? There are a few contenders, but 5esquinas is making a strong claim. It has the full trattoria vibe right down to the open glow of the pizza oven and the aroma of roasted garlic. Visiting Italians won't be disappointed with the seafood pasta (generous on the lobster) or the crab-and-spinach cannelloni. Round it off with tiramisu. (📞7-860-6295; Habana No 104, cnr Cuarteles; mains CUC$5-11; ⏱11am-11pm)

Café Bohemia   TAPAS, CAFE $

16 🍴 Map p34, C6

Inhabiting a beautifully curated mansion on Plaza Vieja, Café Bohemia – named for a Cuban culture and arts magazine – manages to feel appropriately bohemian, but also serves great cocktails, tapas and extremely addictive cakes. (📞7-836-6567; www.havanabohemia.com; San Ignacio No 364; tapas CUC$6-10; ⏱10:30am-9:30pm)

ChaChaChá   INTERNATIONAL $$

17 🍴 Map p34, B4

Spanking new in 2016, ChaChaChá has presented a good opening dance. The food is a smattering of international fare, with early kudos to the

LEMBI/SHUTTERSTOCK ©

El Rum Rum de la Habana (p39)

sizzling fajitas and the well-executed pasta dishes. There's an attractive interior with a mezzanine, retro '50s Mob-era decor, vinyl records serving as place-mats and a bistro-style openfronted location luring people fresh out of the Museo de la Revolución and Bellas Artes. (7-867-2450; Av de las Misiones No 159, btwn Tejadillo & Chacón; mains CUC$7.50-14; noon-2am)

Donde Lis CUBAN $$

18 🍴 Map p34, B4

The Lis' interior is like a modern love letter to Havana: iconography from the Rat Pack era of the 1950s, reproduced 20th-century tropical art and bright colors splashed onto old colonial walls. The menu is a carefully cultivated mélange of different flavors presenting Cuban staples with modern twists – octopus with guacamole, lobster enchilados – along with some Italian and Spanish cameos. (7-860-0922; www.dondelis.com; Tejadillo No 163, btwn Habana & Compostela; mains CUC$5-12; noon-midnight)

Helad'oro ICE CREAM $

19 🍴 Map p34, B4

Back when Fidel was 'king,' the government had a monopoly on many things, including ice cream, which was controlled by the legendary Coppelia and the flavors rarely strayed beyond *fresa y chocolate* (strawberry and chocolate). Then along came the economic defrosting of the 2010s, ushering in Helad'oro with its artisan

ice cream dispensed in 30-plus different flavors, including mamey. Viva the ice-cream revolution! (53-05-91-31; Aguiar No 206, btwn Empredrado & Tejadillo; ice cream CUC$2-4; 11am-10pm)

O'Reilly 304 INTERNATIONAL $$

20 🍴 Map p34, B4

Thinking up the name (the restaurant's address) can't have taken much imagination, so it is perhaps a little ironic that O'Reilly 304 serves up some of the most imaginative cuisine in Havana. Exquisite seafood with crispy veg is presented on metal pans set into wooden trays, while the cocktails and tacos are fast becoming legendary. (52-64-47-25; O'Reilly No 304; meals CUC$8-13; noon-midnight)

Paladar Los Mercaderes CUBAN, INTERNATIONAL $$$

21 🍴 Map p34, D5

This private restaurant in a historic building has to be one of Cuba's most refined paladares for ambience, service and food, both Cuban and international. Follow a staircase strewn with flower petals to a luxurious 1st-floor dining room where musicians play violins and fine international dishes combine meat with exotic sauces. *Muy romántico!* (📞7-861-2437; Mercaderes No 207; meals CUC$12-20; ⏱11am-11pm)

Café del Ángel Fumero Jacqueline   CAFE $

22 🍴 Map p34, B4

Guarding the heavenly small square behind the Iglesia del Santo Ángel Custodio (the result of a foresighted community project), the highly minimalist Fumero is part cocktail bar, part ladies clothing boutique, and also one of the best breakfast spots in Habana Vieja. Pull up an alfresco chair for eggs, waffles and superhot coffee. (📞7-862-6562; Compostela No 1, cnr Cuarteles; breakfast CUC$4-6; ⏱8am-11pm)

Local Life

Restaurante el Templete

Welcome to a rare Cuban breed: a state-run restaurant that can compete with the nascent private sector. The **Templete's** (Map p34, D4; Av Carlos Manuel de Céspedes No 12; mains CUC$15-30; ⏱noon-11pm) specialty is fish, and special it is: fresh, succulent and cooked simply without the pretensions of celebrity-chef-producing nations.

La Vitrola   BREAKFAST, INTERNATIONAL $$

23 🍴 Map p34, C6

A retro '50s place with live music on the corner of Plaza Vieja that routinely gets swamped by tourists in the evening. Unbeknown to many, La Vitrola is actually far better for its quieter alfresco breakfasts of fruit, coffee, toast and generous omelets. (📞52-85-71-11; Muralla No 151, cnr San Ignacio; breakfast CUC$4-7; ⏱8:30am-midnight)

Drinking

El Dandy   BAR, CAFE

24 🍺 Map p34, B6

The jury's still out on Havana's trendiest bar-cafe, but there's little doubt that it's the dandiest. Proving itself to be 'unduly devoted to style, neatness, and fashion in dress and appearance,' El Dandy is a vortex of strong coffee, powerful cocktails and (something not always included in the hipster rule book) warm, unpretentious service. (📞7-867-6463; www.bareldandy.com; cnr Brasil & Villegas; ⏱8am-1am)

Azúcar Lounge   LOUNGE

25 🍺 Map p34, D6

How to make an old square trendy: stick a low-lit, chill-out bar with Ikea-style couches on the upper floor of one of its oldest houses. Sprinkle said bar with avant-garde art and weird light fixtures. Offer lavish cocktails and hypnotic trance music. Call it Azúcar

Understand

Historical Jigsaw

Never in the field of architectural preservation has so much been achieved by so many with so few resources. You hear plenty about the sterling performance of the Cuban education and health-care systems in the international press, but relatively little about the remarkable work that has gone into preserving the country's valuable but seriously endangered historical legacy, most notably in Habana Vieja.

A work in progress since the late 1970s, the piecing back together of Havana's 'old town' after decades of neglect has been a foresighted and startlingly miraculous process considering the economic odds stacked against it. The genius behind the project is Eusebio Leal Spengler, Havana's celebrated City Historian who, unperturbed by the tightening of the financial screws during Cuba's Special Period, set up Habaguanex in 1994, a holding company that earns hard currency through tourism and re-invests it in a mix of historical preservation and city-wide urban regeneration. By safeguarding Havana's historical heritage, Leal and his cohorts have attracted more tourists to the city and earned a bigger slice of revenue for Habaguanex to plough back into further restoration work and much-needed social projects.

Eschewing the temptation to turn Havana's old quarter into a historical theme park, Leal has sought to rebuild the city's urban jigsaw as an authentic 'living' center that provides tangible benefits for the neighborhood's 91,000-plus inhabitants. As a result, schools, neighborhood committees, care-homes for seniors, and centers for children with disabilities sit seamlessly alongside the cleaned-up colonial edifices. Every time you put your money into a Habana Vieja hotel, museum or restaurant, you are contributing, not just to the quarter's continued restoration, but to a whole raft of social projects that directly benefit the local population.

Today, the City Historian's Office splits its annual tourist income (reported to be in excess of US$160 million) between further restoration (45%) and social projects in the city (55%), of which there are now over 400. So far, one quarter of Habana Vieja has been returned to the height of its colonial-era splendor, with ample tourist attractions, including 20 hotels, four classic forts and over 30 museums.

(sugar). (📞7-860-6563; Mercaderes No 315; ⏱11am-midnight)

El Chanchullero   BAR

26 🚇 Map p34, B6

'Aqui jamás estuvo Hemingway' (Hemingway was never here) reads the sign outside roguish Chanchullero, expressing more than a hint of irony. It had to happen. While rich tourists toast Hemingway in La Bodeguita del Medio, hip Cubans and foreigners who think they're hip pay far less for better cocktails in their own boho alternative. (www.el-chanchullero.com; Brasil, btwn Bernaza & Christo; ⏱1pm-midnight)

El Patchanka   BAR

27 🚇 Map p34, B6

Live bands rock the rafters, locals knock back powerful CUC$2 mojitos, and earnest travelers banter about Che Guevara's contribution to modern poster art in this new dive bar in Plaza del Cristo that already looks comfortably lived in. Cultural interaction is the key here. By keeping the prices low (lobster for CUC$6!), Patchanka attracts everyone. (📞7-860-4161; Bernaza No 162; ⏱1pm-1am)

Museo del Chocolate   CAFE

28 🚇 Map p34, D5

Chocolate addicts beware, this unmissable place in Habana Vieja's heart is a lethal dose of chocolate, truffles and yet more chocolate (all made on the premises). Situated – with no irony intended – on Calle Amargura (literally, Bitterness Street), it's more a cafe than a museum, with a small cluster of marble tables set amid a sugary mélange of chocolate paraphernalia. (cnr Amargura & Mercaderes; ⏱9am-9pm)

El Floridita   BAR

29 🚇 Map p34, A5

El Floridita was a favorite of expat Americans long before Hemingway dropped by in the 1930s, hence the name (which means 'Little Florida'). Bartender Constante Ribalaigua invented the daiquiri soon after WWI, but it was Hemingway who popularized it and ultimately the bar christened a drink in his honor: the Papa Hemingway Special (a

---

☑️ Top Tip

José Martí

A basic understanding of Cuban National Hero, José Martí (1853-95) and his far-reaching influence is crucial to understanding contemporary Cuba. Havana, the city of his birth, is dotted with poignant monuments dedicated to the revered poet, journalist, philosopher and all-round Renaissance man. Start at his birth house (p39) in Habana Vieja and follow the legend.

La Bodeguita del Medio

grapefruit-flavored daiquiri). (Obispo No 557; ⏰11am-midnight)

Espacios Old Fashioned   BAR

30 🚇 Map p34, B5

The new offshoot of the hip Miramar restaurant, Espacios inhabits a smaller abode in Habana Vieja, but, like its bigger sibling, adorns its walls with avant-garde art. You can eat here, but we recommend it as a place to sink a glass or cup of something containing caffeine, alcohol or perhaps just juice, while checking out the art – and artists. (📞7-861-3895; www.barrestaurantespaciosoldfashioned.com; Amargura No 258, btwn Habana & Compostela; ⏰noon-midnight)

La Bodeguita del Medio   BAR

31 🚇 Map p34, C4

Made famous thanks to the rum-swilling exploits of Ernest Hemingway (who by association instantly sends the prices soaring), this is Havana's most celebrated bar. A visit here has become de rigueur for tourists who haven't yet cottoned on to the fact that the mojitos are better and (far) cheaper elsewhere. (Empedrado No 207; ⏰11am-midnight)

Bar Dos Hermanos   BAR

32 🚇 Map p34, D6

This once-seedy, now polished bar down by the docks broadcasts a boastful list of former rum-slugging patrons on a plaque by the door: Federico Lorca, Marlon Brando, Errol Flynn and Hemingway (of course) among them. With its long wooden bar and salty seafaring atmosphere, it still spins a little magic. (San Pedro No 304; ⏱24hr)

La Factoria Plaza Vieja BAR

33 🍺 Map p34, C6

Havana's original microbrewery occupies a boisterous corner of Plaza Vieja and sells smooth, cold, homemade beer at sturdy wooden benches set up outside on the cobbles or indoors in a bright, noisy beer hall. Gather a group together and you'll get the amber nectar in a tall plastic tube drawn from a tap at the bottom. There's also an outside grill. (cnr San Ignacio & Muralla; ⏱11am-midnight)

Entertainment

Basílica Menor de San Francisco de Asís CLASSICAL MUSIC

34 ⭐ Map p34, D5

Plaza de San Francisco de Asís' glorious church, which dates from 1738, has been reincarnated as a 21st-century museum and concert hall. The old nave hosts choral and chamber music two to three times a week (check the schedule at the door) and the acoustics

MAURIZIO DE MATTEI/SHUTTERSTOCK ©

Librería Venecia (p47)

inside are famously good. It's best to bag your ticket at least a day in advance. (Plaza de San Francisco de Asís; tickets CUC$3-8; ⏲from 6pm Thu-Sat)

Shopping

Centro Cultural Antiguos Almacenes de Deposito San José

ARTS & CRAFTS

35 Map p34, D7

Havana's open-air handicraft market sits under the cover of an old shipping warehouse in Desamparados. Check your socialist ideals at the door. Herein lies a hive of free enterprise and (unusually for Cuba) haggling. Possible souvenirs include paintings, *guayabera* shirts, woodwork, leather items, jewelry and numerous apparitions of the highly marketable El Che. (cnr Desamparados & San Ignacio; ⏲10am-6pm Mon-Sat)

Clandestina

CLOTHING

36 Map p34, B6

Progressive private shops are still in their infancy in Havana, but this is one of the best, set up by a Cuban artist in the mid-2010s and selling its clothes (many of them recycled), bags and accessories under the banner '99% Cuban design'. Viva the private boutique. (☎53-81-48-02; Villegas No 403; ⏲10am-8pm)

Local Life

Plaza de Armas Secondhand Book Market

A long-standing **secondhand book market** (Map p34, D4; cnr Obispo & Tacón; ⏲9am-7pm) convenes under the leafy boughs in Plaza de Armas most days. It stocks old, new and rare books, including Hemingway, some weighty poetry and plenty of written pontifications from Fidel. There's no market on rainy days or on important holidays.

Casa del Habano – Hostal Conde de Villanueva

CIGARS

37 Map p34, C5

One of Havana's best cigar shops, with its own roller, smoking room and expert sales staff. (Mercaderes No 202; ⏲10am-6pm)

Librería Venecia

BOOKS

38 Map p34, B5

A nice little private secondhand bookshop in Obispo where you might uncover all number of mysteries. It's particularly good for its old Cuban posters, which steer clear of the clichéd Che Guevara poses. (Obispo No 502; ⏲10am-10pm)

Explore

Centro Habana

On Centro Habana's pot-holed but perennially action-packed streets, old men engage in marathon games of dominoes, Afro-Cuban drums beat out addictive rumba rhythms and sorrily soiled buildings give intriguing hints of their illustrious previous lives. Juxtaposed against this ebullient but spectacularly dilapidated quarter is the tourist-heavy zone around Parque Central full of posh hotels and fine museums.

The Sights in a Day

In Centro Habana all roads lead to action-packed **Parque Central** (p59), ground zero for exploratory forays into the neighborhood and a veritable piece of outdoor theater surrounded by some of Havana's most important buildings. Take time to examine the **Gran Teatro de la Habana Alicia Alonso** (p63; pictured left), the Centro Asturianos and the skyline-hogging **Capitolio Nacional** (p58). Heading north, wander down the tree-lined walkway on **El Prado** (p54) to get orientated.

Dedicate the first part of the afternoon to the fabulous **Museo Nacional de Bellas Artes** (p50), then press on down El Prado into the **Malecón** (p55), Havana's elongated sea drive that's worth checking out at different times of day. To the south and easily accessible is Centro Habana's clamorous residential grid. If you want an in-your-face, warts-and-all taste of real Havana, this is it. Stop for coffee in **Café Arcangel** (p62) and dive into the **Barrio Chino** (p55), one of the world's more unusual 'Chinatowns'.

Dine in luxuriant **San Cristóbal** (p60) and down a dark rum in **Sloppy Joe's** (p62) before heading over to **El Guajirito** (p65) for a night of unashamed son-salsa nostalgia

For a local's day in Centro Habana, see p54.

Top Sights

Museo Nacional de Bellas Artes (p50)

Museo de la Revolución (p52)

Local Life

Centro Habana Streetlife (p54)

Best of Havana

Nightlife

Gran Teatro de la Habana Alicia Alonso (p63)

Casa de la Música (p65)

El Guajirito (p65)

Art & Architecture

Museo Nacional de Bellas Artes (p50)

Callejón de Hamel (p55)

Capitolio Nacional (p58)

Convento & Iglesia del Carmen (p60)

Getting There & Away

Bus Parque de la Fraternidad is Centro Habana's main transport nexus, with metro buses fanning out all over the city. Parque Central is the main interchange for the Habana Bus Tour routes T1 and T3.

Top Sights
Museo Nacional de Bellas Artes

Spread over two campuses, the Bellas Artes is arguably the finest art gallery in the Caribbean. The 'Arte Cubano' building contains the most comprehensive collection of Cuban art in the world, while the 'Arte Universal' section is laid out in a grand eclectic palace overlooking Parque Central, with exterior flourishes that are just as impressive as the art within.

⊙ Map p56, G2

www.bellasartes.cult.cu

Each gallery CUC$5, combined entry to both CUC$8, under 14yr free

⊙9am-5pm Tue-Sat, 10am-2pm Sun

Arte Cubano Collection

The Cuban collection is exhibited in the original museum building dating from 1955. Works are displayed in chronological order starting on the 3rd floor and are surprisingly varied. Artists to look out for include Guillermo Collazo, considered to be the first truly great Cuban artist, Rafael Blanco, with his cartoon-like paintings and sketches, Raúl Martínez, a master of 1960s Cuban pop art, and the Picasso-like Wifredo Lam.

Arte Universal Collection

Since 2001, the international collection displaying art from 500 BC to the present day has been exhibited on three separate floors of the Palacio de los Asturianos. Its undisputed highlight is its Spanish collection, with some canvases by Zurburïán, Murillo and de Ribera, and a tiny Velázquez. Also worth perusing are the 2000-year-old Roman mosaics, Greek pots from the 5th century BC, and a suitably refined Gainsborough canvas (in the British room).

La Gitana Tropical

Sometimes dubbed the 'Mona Lisa of the Caribbean,' this simple but haunting study of a Latino woman by Havana-born painter Victor Manuel García Valdés was executed in Paris in 1929 and shows distinct European influences. Valdés was part of the Vanguardia movement of artists and his *Gitana* isn't just the country's most cherished painting, it also serves as a precursor to Cuban modernism.

☑ **Top Tips**

▶ If you're short on time, admire the Centro Asturianos from the outside and the more topical (and tropical) Arte Cubano collection from within.

▶ Buying a joint ticket for CUC$8 will save you CUC$2.

▶ There's lots to see. Reserve a good 90 minutes for both museums.

✗ **Take a Break**

It's not at all sloppy and Joe no longer works there, but Sloppy Joe's (p62) does a mean spicy beef sandwich. Alternatively, you can dance across to ChaChaChá (p40), a new restaurant with an international menu.

Top Sights
Museo de la Revolución

Laid out in one of Havana's finest palaces, this museum tracks Cuba's history from pre-Columbian culture to the present socialist regime with a strong focus – as the name implies – on the revolution and its aftermath, Despite the inevitable propaganda, the displays provide a good starting point for anyone keen to understand Cuba's recent history.

◉ Map p56, G2

Refugio No 1

CUC$8, guided tours CUC$2

◷9:30am-4pm

Museum Chronology

The museum exhibits descend chronologically from the top floor, focusing primarily on the events leading up to, during, and immediately after the Cuban revolution. It presents a some-times scruffy but always compelling story told in English and Spanish, and tinted with *mucho* propaganda. Black-and-white photos, maps and occasional revolutionary mementos color the displays.

Second Floor Rooms

The palace's sweeping central staircase takes you up to the 2nd floor and several important exhibit-free rooms, including the **Salón Dorado** (decorated in Louis VI style and once used for banquets), the **Despacho Presidencial** (presi-dent's office where Fidel Castro was sworn in in 1959), and the **capilla** (chapel, with a Tiffany chandelier).

Pavillón Granma

In the space behind the museum you'll find the Pavillón Granma, a memorial to the 18m yacht that carried Fidel Castro and 81 other revolution-aries from Tuxpán, Mexico, to Cuba in December 1956. It's encased in glass and guarded 24 hours a day, presumably to stop anyone from breaking in and sailing off to Florida in it. The pavilion is surrounded by other vehicles associated with the revolution, including planes, rockets and an old postal van used as a getaway car in 1957 during an unsuccessful attack on the presidential palace by a group of university students led by José Antonio Echeverría, intent on assassinating President Fulgenicio Batista.

FOROV/SHUTTERSTOCK ©

☑ Top Tips

▶ Start at the top of the palace and work down so you can follow the correct historical chronology.

▶ The Pavillón Granma can only be accessed through the museum. Don't try to get a peep from the streets or guards will curtly usher you away.

▶ Guided tours cost an extra CUC$2.

✗ Take a Break

The museum has a small ground-floor cafe, but, for refreshment, you're better off heading across Av de las Mis-iones to the Plazuela de Santo Ángel behind the Santo Ángel Custodio church, where there are several good cafes with outdoor tables.

Local Life
Centro Habana Streetlife

Life in Centro Habana goes on irrespective of tourism, inclement weather or the distractions of the internet age. During the day, this ebullient but dilapidated neighborhood is a microcosm of Cuban life, the city's most densely populated district with 140,000 people squeezed into a 3-sq-km grid. At night it resembles a shady, old-fashioned movie set.

❶ El Prado

On weekends the tree-shaded European-style walkway that cuts down the center of **Paseo de Martí (El Prado)** is filled with Cuban artists producing, displaying and selling their work. The rest of the week you can practice your side-stepping skills with soccer-playing kids and school teachers holding PE classes.

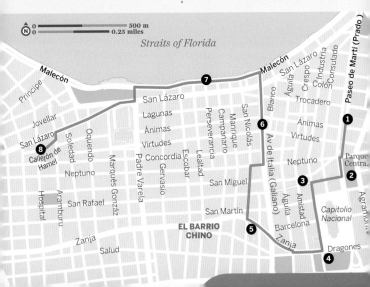

❷ Esquina Caliente

Follow the shouts emanating from the omnipresent group of Cuban men who stand arguing boisterously near the José Martí statue in Parque Central. The topic of conversation is generally baseball, and the melee is known as the Esquina Caliente ('hot corner'), after the corner of Calles 23 and 12 in Vedado where it originally convened.

❸ El Bulevar

Pedestrianized Calle San Rafael, near the Hotel Inglaterra, is an unashamedly local affair, with peso snack stalls, half-bare grocery shops and 1950s shopping nostalgia. As in other Cuban cities, shoppers refer to it as **El Bulevar** (San Rafael, btwn Paseo de Martí & Av de Italia).

❹ Parque de la Fraternidad

Want a picture of one of those old American cars? Dozens of colectivos (communal taxis) wait in line around the Capitolio in what has been dubbed 'Jurassic Park.' The park's real name, **Parque de la Fraternidad**, is meant to signify American brotherhood, hence the many busts of American leaders that embellish the green areas, including Abraham Lincoln.

❺ El Barrio Chino

Havana's **El Barrio Chino** is notable for its lack of Chinese people, most of whom left as soon as a newly inaugu-

rated Fidel Castro uttered the word '*socialismo.*' However in the 1990s, the Cuban government recognized the tourist potential of the area; recently it has invested money and resources into rejuvenating the district's distinct historical character.

❻ Calle Galiano

The street officially called Av de Italia is still referred to by *habaneros* as Calle Galiano. Serving as Centro Habana's main drag, it was once lined with plush department stores. These days the demeanor is more downbeat, although the action is just as lively.

❼ Malecón

Get a glimpse of the real, uncensored Cuba on Havana's sea wall, where hundreds of *habaneros* come to stroll at sunset. The 7km-long **Malecón** is a quintessential Havana experience, a giant outdoor living room packed with fishers, lovers, musicians, joggers, jokers and dreamy Florida-gazers.

❽ Callejón de Hamel

That cauldron full of old sticks is called a *nganga* (a Palo Monte altar) and those people dressed in white are *Iyabós* (Santería initiates). Welcome to **Callejón de Hamel** (⊙from noon Sun), the paint-splattered back alley that acts as a center for Havana's Afro-Cuban culture and is rightly famous for its free outdoor rumba drummers.

A B C D

1

For reviews see

N 0 ___ 400 m
0 ___ 0.2 miles

Malecón (Av de Maceo)

C 23
C P
Humboldt
Calz de la Infanta
CO
CN
C 25
Príncipe
Vapor
Jovellar

2

CAYO HUESO

San Lázaro
Lagunas
Ánimas
Escobar
Lealtad
15

Hospital Nacional Hermanos Ameijeiras

C 27
Av Universidad
San Lázaro
Callejón de Hamel
Soledad
Virtudes
Concordia
Gervasio
Virtudes
Concordia
12
Padre Varela
Lucena
Marqués Gonzáz

3

San Lázaro
Neptuno
San Miguel
San Rafael
San Martín

San Francisco
Espada
Hospital
Aramburu

Neptuno
San Miguel
San Rafael
San Martín

Neptuno
San Miguel
San Rafael
San Martín
Zanja

4

Calz de Zapata

Zanja
Salud
Soledad
Pocito

Padre Varela
Santiago
Gervasio

Pocito

5

Av Salvador Allende
Calz de la Infanta

Luaces
Calz de Ayestarán

Bruzón

Enrique Barnet
Retiro
Maloja
Sitio
Peñalver

Oquendo
Marqués Gonzáz
San Carlos
Escobar
Lealtad

Real Fábrica de Tabacos Partagás
8

Castillo de San Salvador de laPunta

Straits of Florida

E **F** **G** **H**

1

⊗13

Av de los Estudiantes

Cárcel

◉7

Parque de los Enamorados

⊗11

Genios

Agramonte

Tacón

Cuba

Aguiar

Malecón

San Lázaro

Aguila

Crespo

Refugio

Paseo de Martí (Prado)

Museo de la Revolución ◉

Chacón

Av de las Misiones

Aguacate

Compostela

Tejadillo

Empedrado

20 ◙

⊗10

Blanco

Av de Italia (Galiano)

Trocadero

Colón

2

14

San Nicolás

Bernal

Ánimas

Industria

Consulado

Museo Nacional de Bellas Artes ◉

Habana

Aguiar

Perseverancia

Campanario

Manrique

Virtudes

24 19

San Juan de Dios

O'Reilly

Obispo

Neptuno

23 ◙17

☆

21

Amistad

Hotel **4** Inglaterra ◉

6 ◉

Parque Central

San Martín

Obrapía

Lamparilla

3

San Miguel

San Rafael

Gran Teatro de la Habana Alicia Alonso

2 ◉

Brasil

Cristo

Villegas

Aguacate

Compostela

Muralla

⊗ 9

EL BARRIO CHINO

Cuchillo

16

Dragones

Aguila

Av de Italia (Galiano)

1 ◉

Barcelona

18 ◙

Capitolio Nacional

25 ◙

Paseo de Martí (Prado)

Agramonte

Bernaza

Sol

Luz

4

Salud

Zanja

Dragones

Asociación Cultural Yoruba de Cuba ◉**3**

Av de Bélgica

Acosta

Jesús María

Merced

Picota

Av Simón Bolívar

Enrique Barnet

Parque El Curita

Campanario

Manrique

San Nicolás

Rayo

Maloja

Máximo Gómez

Aguila

Revillagigedo

Sitio

Factoría

Súarez

Corrales

Apodaca

Aponte

Cárdenas

Cienfuegos

Economía

◉**22**

5

Peñalver

Indio

Gloria

Misión

Estación Central de Ferrocarriles (Central Train Station) ◉

Old City Wall ◉**5**

Sights

Capitolio Nacional   LANDMARK

1  Map p56, F4

The incomparable Capitolio Nacional is Havana's most ambitious and grandiose building, constructed after the post-WWI sugar boom ('Dance of the Millions') gifted the Cuban government a seemingly bottomless bank vault of sugar money. Similar to the Capitol building in Washington, DC, but actually modeled on the Panthéon in Paris, the building was initiated by Cuba's US-backed dictator Gerardo Machado in 1926 and took 5000 workers three years, two months and 20 days to construct at a cost of US$17 million. (cnr Dragones & Paseo de Martí)

Gran Teatro de la Habana Alicia Alonso   THEATER

2  Map p56, G3

The original ornate neobaroque **Centro Gallego** was erected as a Galician social club between 1907 and 1914. Standing the test of time, the theater was renovated in 2015 and now sparkles afresh from its perch in Parque Central. Ask about guided tours at the box office. (Paseo de Martí No 458)

Gran Teatro de la Habana Alicia Alonso

Asociación Cultural Yoruba de Cuba

MUSEUM

3 ⊙ Map p56, G4

To untangle the confusing mysteries of the Santería religion, its saints and their powers, decamp to this museum-cum-cultural-center. Aside from sculpted models of the various *orishas* (deities), the association also hosts *tambores* (Santería drum ceremonies) on Friday and Saturday at 6pm (CUC$5). Check the noticeboard at the door. Note that there's a church dress code for the *tambores* (no shorts or tank tops). (Paseo de Martí No 615; CUC$5; ⊙9am-4:30pm Mon-Sat)

Hotel Inglaterra

HISTORIC BUILDING

4 ⊙ Map p56, G3

Havana's oldest hotel first opened its doors in 1856 on the site of a popular bar called El Louvre (the hotel's alfresco bar still bears the name). Facing leafy Parque Central, the building exhibits the neoclassical design features in vogue at the time, complemented by a lobby beautified with Moorish tiles. At a banquet here in 1879, José Martí made a speech advocating Cuban independence, and much later US journalists covering the Spanish-American War stayed at the hotel. (Paseo de Martí No 416)

Old City Wall

HISTORIC SITE

5 ⊙ Map p56, H5

In the 17th century, anxious to defend the city from attacks by pirates and overzealous foreign armies, Cuba's paranoid colonial authorities drew up plans for the construction of a 5km-long city wall. Built between 1674 and 1740, the wall on completion was 1.5m thick and 10m high, running along a line now occupied by Av de las Misiones and Av de Bélgica.

Parque Central

PARK

6 ⊙ Map p56, G3

Diminutive Parque Central is a verdant haven from the belching buses and roaring taxis that ply their way along Paseo de Martí (Prado). The park, long a microcosm of daily Havana life, was expanded to its present size in the late 19th century after the city walls were knocked down. The 1905 marble **statue of José Martí** at its center was the first of thousands to be erected in Cuba.

Parque de los Enamorados

PARK

7 ⊙ Map p56, G1

In Parque de los Enamorados (Lovers' Park), surrounded by streams of speeding traffic, lies a surviving section of the colonial **Cárcel** (aka Tacón Prison), built in 1838, where many Cuban patriots, including José Martí, were imprisoned. A brutal place that sent prisoners to perform hard labor in the nearby San Lázaro quarry, it was demolished in 1939, with this park dedicated to the memory of those who had suffered so horribly within its walls. Two tiny cells and a chapel are all that remain.

Real Fábrica de Tabacos Partagás

FACTORY

8 ⊙ Map p56, D5

One of Havana's oldest and most famous cigar factories, the landmark Real Fábrica de Tabacos Partagás was founded in 1845 by Spaniard Jaime Partagás. Since 2013, the factory has moved from its original building behind the Capitolio to this location just off Calle Padre Varela in Centro Habana. Tickets for factory tours must be bought beforehand in the lobby of the Hotel Saratoga (p145). (San Carlos No 816, btwn Peñalver & Sitios; tours CUC$10; ⊙tours every 15min 9am-1pm Mon-Fri)

Local Life
Convento & Iglesia del Carmen

The little-visited **Convento & Iglesia del Carmen** (Map p56, A3; cnr Calzada de la Infanta & Neptuno; ⊙7:30am-noon & 3-7pm Tue-Sun) sports a craning bell-tower that dominates the Centro Habana skyline and is topped by a huge statue of Nuestra Señora del Carmen, but the real prizes lie inside: rich Seville-style tiles, a gilded altarpiece, ornate woodcarving and swirling frescoes. Surprisingly, the church was only built in 1923 to house the Carmelite order. The building is considered 'eclectic.'

Eating

San Cristóbal

CUBAN $$$

9 ✕ Map p56, E3

San Cristóbal was knocking out fine food long before the leader of the free world dropped by in March 2016, although the publicity garnered from President Obama's visit probably helped. Crammed into one of Centro Habana's grubbier streets, the restaurant has a museum-worthy interior crowded with old photos, animal skins, and a Santería altar flanked by pictures of Maceo and Martí. (☑7-867-9109; San Rafael, btwn Campanario & Lealtad; meals CUC$9-18; ⊙noon-midnight Mon-Sat)

Castas y Tal

CUBAN $$

10 ✕ Map p56, F2

In its short life the C&T has gone from old-school paladar (ensconced in someone's 11th-floor apartment) to trendy bistro-style restaurant. High-quality and adventurous food, such as lamb with Indian masala, or chicken in orange sauce, comes backed up with Cuban classics (lashing of rice and beans are served on the side). It's all beautifully presented, too. (☑7-864-2177; Av de Italia No 51, cnr San Lázaro; mains CUC$6-9; ⊙noon-midnight)

Castropol

SPANISH $$

11 ✕ Map p56, F1

Castropol is run by the local Spanish Asturianas society, and its reputation has expanded in line with its fleshed-out restaurant space over the last few years. Word is now out that the venerable two-story establishment, with its upstairs balcony overlooking Havana's dreamy sea drive, serves some of the best Spanish and Caribbean food in Havana. (📞7-861-4864; Malecón 107, btwn Genios & Crespo; mains CUC$9-20; ⏱6pm-midnight)

La Guarida   INTERNATIONAL $$$
12 ✕ Map p56, D3

Only in Havana! The entrance to the city's most legendary private restaurant greets you like a scene out of a 1940s film noir. A decapitated statue at the bottom of a grand but dilapidated staircase leads up past lines of drying clothes to a wooden door, behind which lie multiple culinary surprises. (📞7-866-9047; www.laguarida.com; Concordia No 418, btwn Gervasio & Escobar; mains CUC$15-22; ⏱noon-3pm & 7pm-midnight)

Nazdarovie   RUSSIAN $$
13 ✕ Map p56, G1

Cuba's 31-year dalliance with bolshevism is relived in this new and highly popular restaurant in prime digs overlooking the Malecón. Upstairs, the decor is awash with old Soviet propaganda posters, brotherly photos of Fidel and Khrushchev and slightly less bombastic Russian dolls. The menu is in three languages (to get in the real spirit, try ordering in Russian). (📞7-860-2947; www.nazdarovie-havana.com; Malecón No 25, btwn Prado & Cárcel; mains CUC$10-12; ⏱noon-midnight)

☑ Top Tip

Tours in Classic American Cars

One of Havana's first private tour companies, **Havana Super Tour** (Map p56, E2; 📞52-65-71-01; www.campanario63.com; Campanario No 63, btwn San Lázaro & Lagunas; tours CUC$35) runs all its trips in classic American cars. The two most popular are the art deco architectural tour and the 'Mob tour,' uncovering the city's pre-revolution Mafia haunts. If you're short on time, the full-blown Havana day tour (CUC$150) will whip you around all of the city's key sights.

Casa Abel   INTERNATIONAL $$
14 ✕ Map p56, E2

Rum and cigars dominate the proceedings at Casa Abel. Several food dishes on the menu contain meats marinated in Cuba's favorite tipple (including chicken marinated in rum and then smoke-roasted with beer!), while on the floor above the dining room you can puff away till your heart's content (or lament) in a smoking room, with *puros* (cigars) chosen from a special menu. (📞7-860-6589; San Lázaro No 319, cnr San Nicolás; mains CUC$7-16; ⏱noon-midnight)

Casa Miglis   SWEDISH $$
15 ✕ Map p56, D2

There's a place for everything in Havana these days, even Swedish-Cuban fusion food. Emerging improbably from a kitchen in the battle-scarred tenements of Centro Habana, comes *toast skagen* (prawns on toast), ceviche, couscous, and the *crème de la crème*: melt-in-your-mouth meatballs with mashed potato. (☑7-864-1486; www.casamiglis.com; Lealtad No 120, btwn Ánimas & Lagunas; mains CUC$6-12; ⊗noon-1am)

Restaurante Tien-Tan   CHINESE $$

16 🍴 Map p56, E4

One of Barrio Chino's best authentic Chinese restaurants, Tien-Tan ('Temple of Heaven') is run by a Chinese-Cuban couple and serves up an incredible 130 different dishes. Try chop suey with vegetables or chicken with cashew nuts and sit outside in action-packed Cuchillo, one of Havana's most colorful and fastest-

---

Local Life
Los Nardos

An open secret opposite the Capitolio, but easy to miss (look out for the queue), **Los Nardos** (Map p56, G4; ☑7-863-2985; Paseo de Martí No 563; mains CUC$4-10; ⊗noon-midnight) is a semi-private restaurant operated by the Spanish Asturianas society. The dilapidated exterior promises little, but the leather/mahogany decor and generous-sized dishes inside suggest otherwise – Los Nardos is touted in some quarters as one of the best cheap eateries in the city.

---

growing 'food streets.' (☑7-863-2081; Cuchillo No 17, btwn Rayo & San Nicolás; meals CUC$7-12; ⊗10:30am-11pm)

Drinking

Café Arcangel   CAFE

17 ☕ Map p56, F3

Excellent coffee, fine *tortas* (cakes), suave non-reggaeton music and Charlie Chaplin movies playing on a loop in a scarred Centro Habana apartment – what more could you want? (☑5-268-5451; Concordia No 57; ⊗8:30am-6:30pm Mon-Sat, 8:15am-1pm Sun)

Sia Kara Café   BAR

18 ☕ Map p56, F4

Located behind the Capitolio in an otherwise completely ungentrified area of Old Havana, Sia Kara is a fun spot day or night – stop in during the afternoon to relax with a book, or enjoy live music and cocktails in the evenings. The ambience is warm, and the kitchen serves up tasty tapas. Service can be spotty, but it's definitely worth a visit. (☑7-867-4084; www.facebook.com/siakaracafecuba; Calle Barcelona, cnr Calle Industria No. 502; ⊗noon-2am Mon-Sun)

Sloppy Joe's   BAR

19 ☕ Map p56, G3

This bar, opened by young Spanish immigrant José García (aka 'Joe') in 1919, earned its name due to its dodgy sanitation and a soggy *ropa vieja*

Sloppy Joe's (p62)

(shredded-beef) sandwich. Legendary among expats before the revolution, it closed in the '60s after a fire, but was reincarnated in 2013 beneath the same noble neoclassical facade. And it's still serving decent cocktails and soggy sandwiches. (cnr Agramonte & Ánimas; ☾noon-3am)

Café Neruda   BAR

20 ⊖ Map p56, E2

A romantically disheveled place on the Malecón, named after the famous Chilean man of letters, Pablo Neruda, this cafe is better for its drinks than its food menu. Spend a poetic after-noon writing your own verse as the waves splash over the sea wall. (Ma-lecón No 203, btwn Manrique & San Nicolás; ☾11am-11pm)

Entertainment

Gran Teatro de la Habana Alicia Alonso   THEATER

Havana's fabulously renovated 'great' theater (see 2 ◉ Map p56, G3) is open again and offering up the best in Cuban dance and music. Its specialty is ballet (it's the headquarters of the Cuban National Ballet), but it also stages musicals, plays and opera. Check the noticeboard for upcoming events. (📞7-861-3077; cnr Paseo de Martí & San Rafael; per person CUC$20; ☾box office 9am-6pm Mon-Sat, to 3pm Sun)

Understand

The Vanguardia

The first real flowering of Cuban art took place in the 1920s when a group of young painters rejecting the orthodoxy of Havana's San Alejandro Academy came together in a loose group known as the 'Vanguardia.' The Vanguardia hungrily absorbed influences from contemporary Paris, where many of the artists had spent time living and working in close proximity to European avant-gardists like Pablo Picasso. Surrealism, cubism and primitivism all began to seep into Cuban art during this period, but it was counterbalanced by inherently Cuban themes such as Santería and indigenous culture. One of the Vanguardia's earliest exponents was Victor Manuel García (1897–1969), the genius behind Cuba's most famous painting, *La Gitana Tropical* (Tropical Gypsy; 1929).

Victor Manuel's contemporary, Amelia Peláez (1896–1968), the only female member of the Vanguardia, also studied in Paris, where she melded avant-gardism with more traditional Cuban themes. Although Peláez labored in many different genres, her most important work was in murals. Her gigantic 670-sq-m *Frutas Cubanas* (Cuban Fruit; 1957) dominates the facade of the Hotel Habana Libre.

Another member of the Vanguardia was Rene Portocarrero (1912–85), a Havana-born artist who left the San Alejandro Academy while he was still in his teens in order to allow himself a more free-flowing approach to ceramics, painting and stained-glass design. His abstract work shows strong hints of Santería and Cuban legend.

In an objective sense, Cuban art reached its apex with Wifredo Lam (1902–82), a painter, sculptor and ceramicist of mixed Chinese, African and Spanish ancestry. Born in Sagua La Grande, Villa Clara province, in 1902, Lam studied art and law in Havana before departing for Madrid in 1923 to pursue his artistic ambitions in the fertile fields of post-WWI Europe. Displaced by the Spanish Civil War in 1937, he gravitated toward France, where he became friends with Pablo Picasso and swapped ideas with the pioneering surrealist André Breton. Having absorbed various cubist and surrealist influences, Lam returned to Cuba in 1941, where he produced his own seminal masterpiece *La Jungla* (Jungle; 1943), considered by critics to be one of the developing world's most representative paintings.

Casa de la Música
LIVE MUSIC

21 ⭐ Map p56, F3

One of Cuba's best and most popular nightclubs and live-music venues. All the big names play here, from Bamboleo to Los Van Van – and you'll pay peanuts to see them. Of the city's two Casas de la Música, this Centro Habana version is a little edgier than its Miramar counterpart (some say it's too edgy), with big salsa bands and not much space. (Av de Italia, btwn Concordia & Neptuno; CUC$5-25; ⏰5pm-3am)

El Guajirito
LIVE MUSIC

22 ⭐ Map p56, G5

Some label it a tourist trap, but this restaurant-cum-entertainment-space bivouacked upstairs in a deceptively dilapidated Havana tenement plays some of the most professional Buena Vista Social Club music you'll ever hear. Indeed, this is a Buena Vista Social Club of sorts. (📞7-863-3009; Agramonte No 660, btwn Gloria & Apodeca; show CUC$30; ⏰9:30pm)

Teatro América
THEATER

23 ⭐ Map p56, F3

Housed in a classic art deco *rascacielo* (skyscraper) on Av de Italia (Galiano), the América seems to have changed little since its theatrical heyday in the 1930s and '40s. It plays host to variety, comedy, dance, jazz and salsa; shows are normally held on Saturday at 8:30pm and Sunday at 5pm. (Av de Italia No 253, btwn Concordia & Neptuno)

Shopping

Memorias Librería
BOOKS

24 🔒 Map p56, G3

A shop full of beautiful old artifacts, the Memorias Librería opened in 2014 as Havana's first genuine antique bookstore. Delve into its gathered piles and you'll find wonderful rare collectibles, including old coins, postcards, posters, magazines and art deco signs from the 1930s. Priceless! (📞7-862-3153; Ánimas No 57, btwn Paseo de Martí & Agramonte; ⏰9am-5pm)

Real Fábrica de Tabacos Partagás
CIGARS

25 🔒 Map p56, F4

Confusingly, the cigar shop affiliated with Havana's main cigar factory is still housed here on the ground floor of the original building behind the Capitolio; the factory (p60) itself has moved a couple of kilometers away. Naturally, it sells some of Havana's best smokes. (Industria No 520, btwn Barcelona & Dragones; ⏰9am-7pm)

ALMA MATER

Explore

Vedado

Majestic, spread-out Vedado is Havana's once-notorious Mafia-run district. During Cuba's 50-year dalliance with the US, this was the city's commercial hub and, in many ways, it still is; although these days the nightlife is less tawdry, the casinos have become discos, and the hotels seem more like historical relics than havens of luxury.

The Sights in a Day

☀️ A good orientation point in Vedado is the corner of Calles 23 and L next to the **Hotel Habana Libre** (p76). Check what's on at **Cine Yara** (p71) and perhaps savor an early ice cream at the **Coppelia** (p70) before heading over to the **Universidad de la Habana** (p74; pictured left) to enjoy a leafy erudite atmosphere and check out the **Museo Napoleónico** (p74) opposite.

☀️ Load up in **Waoo Snack Bar** (p80) before appreciating Vedado's famus hotel quarter dominated by the emblematic **Hotel Nacional** (p74). Bisect the neighborhood on attractive tree-lined Calle 17 stopping to relish grand **Av de los Presidentes** (p75) and the even grander **Museo de Artes Decorativas** (p74). Check out the matinees at **Submarino Amarillo** (p71) and have your photo taken in **Parque Lennon** (p77) before hitting the not-to-be-missed **Necrópolis Cristóbal Colón** (p68), which is best viewed near sunset (last entry 5pm).

🌙 Partake in a fusion dinner at **Versus 1900** (p78) before gravitating upstairs to the aptly named rooftop bar **Chill Out** (p81). Imbibe a warm-up cocktail and then head west for one of the city's best nights out at **Fábrica de Arte Cubano** (p83).

For a local's night out in Vedado, see p70.

👁 Top Sights

Necrópolis Cristóbal Colón (p68)

🔍 Local Life

Vedado by Night (p70)

💜 Best of Havana

Eating

Café Laurent (p77)

Starbien (p77)

El Idilio (p79)

La Chuchería (p79)

El Biky (p79)

La Torre (p79)

Drinking

Café Madrigal (p80)

Café Mamainé (p80)

Chill Out (p81)

Café Presidente (p77)

Getting There & Away

🚌 **Bus** The Habana Bus Tour T1 stops at Plaza de la Revolución, Hotel Riviera and the Necrópolis Cristóbal Colón.

🚗 **Car** Taxis tend to wait around outside the main hotels, including the Hotel Nacional and the Hotel Habana Libre.

Top Sights
Necrópolis Cristóbal Colón

Havana's gigantic cemetery is the finest in the Americas and rightly renowned for its striking religious iconography and elaborate marble statues. Far from being eerie, a walk through these 57 hallowed hectares can be an educational and emotional stroll through the annals of Cuban history. A detailed map is available at the entrance.

◉ Map p72, D5

CUC$5

⏱ 8am-6pm, last entry 5pm

Puerta de la Paz

The main entrance, better known as the Puerta de la Paz (Peace Gate) is framed by a splendid Byzantine-Romanesque triple arch that's topped by a statue of Our Lady of Mercy, carved by Cuban sculptor José Villalta Saavedra in 1904.

The Vital Statistics

Completed in 1871 using the designs of Spanish architect Calixto de Loira, the cemetery is one of the world's largest, harboring over 450 mausoleums and 800,000 graves. Around 1.5 million living souls visit it annually and people are buried here at the rate of around 50 per day.

Capilla Central

The neo-Romanesque Capilla Central (1886) located in the dead center of the cemetery is an unusual octagonal construction said to be modeled on Florence's Duomo. Rare is the day when you don't see at least one solemn funeral procession filing out of its hushed interior.

La Milagrosa

Just northeast of the Capilla Central is the graveyard's most celebrated (and visited) tomb, that of Señora Amelia Goyri, better known as La Milagrosa (the miraculous one), who died while giving birth on May 3, 1901. When the bodies were exhumed some years later, Amelia's body was uncorrupted (a sign of sanctity in the Catholic faith) and the baby, who had been buried at its mother's feet, was allegedly found in her arms. As a result, La Milagrosa became the focus of a huge spiritual cult in Cuba, and thousands of people come here annually with gifts, in the hope of fulfilling dreams or solving problems.

☑ Top Tips

▶ If you're short on time, stick to the main sights along Av Cristóbal Colón between Puerta de la Paz and Capilla Central.

▶ Detailed maps marked with all the important graves are available from the ticket office for CUC$1.

▶ The cemetery is particularly beautiful and tranquil at sunset.

▶ Free guided tours leave regularly from the ticket office when there are enough people.

✕ Take a Break

There's not much of note in the immediate vicinity of the cemetery. For a quick drink, wander over to Café Fresa y Chocolate (p71) on Calle 23. A little further away, but worth the walk, is cool and trendy Café Madrigal (p80).

Local Life
Vedado by Night

'Two fatherlands, have I; Cuba and the Night' once wrote José Martí. Beneath the well-feted nightspots of Havana lies a parallel universe of less heavily promoted bars and venues for which you may need a Spanish phrasebook, an 'in' with a Cuban *amigo,* and a mixture of luck and spontaneity.

① Coppelia

Despite the surge in tourist numbers in recent years, the ice-cream parlor **Coppelia** (cnr Calles 23 & L; ice cream from MN$40; ⊙10am-9:30pm Tue-Sat), slap-bang in the middle of commercial Vedado, remains a quintessentially local stronghold. Perhaps the intricacies of the queueing and serving system put people off – suffice to say, with some Cuban pesos and a few words of Spanish you'll be warmly welcomed into the fold.

2 Cine Yara

Cinemas are popular in Cuba, a country where North American TV has yet to dominate. The **Cine Yara** (cnr Calles 23 & L) is arguably Havana's finest, the host to many a Cuban date night, and a good place to wise up to the nation's dynamic film culture while fine-tuning your Spanish.

3 Café Teatro Bertolt Brecht

Ask any young *habanero* about where they go on Wednesday nights, and they'll probably mention the **'Brecht'** (🖉7-832-9359; cnr Calles 13 & I; tickets CUC$3), where long queues file patiently into an intimate theater to see genre-bending Cuban music collective Interactivo spin a couple of hours of melodic magic.

4 El Hurón Azul

The home of the Union of Cuban Writers and Artists (Uneac), **El Hurón Azul** (🖉7-832-4551; www.uneac.org.cu; cnr Calles 17 & H; ⊘hours vary) pulls in the local literati on Saturday nights for its long-standing *bolero* shows. You can mingle freely with the pretentious and precocious in a grand Vedado mansion amid decorative architecture and whispering plants with barely a tourist on the horizon.

5 Submarino Amarillo

No one knew much about Cuban *roqueros* (rock fans) until relatively recently. The groups who used to hang out clandestinely on the corner of Calles 23 and G have subsequently founded their own venue, **Submarino Amarillo** (cnr Calles 17 & 6; ⊘2-7:30pm & 9pm-2am Tue-Sat, 2-10pm Sun, 9pm-2am Mon), a bar-cum-live-music-club with a bright yellow interior that celebrates The Beatles, but rocks to pretty much anything in 4/4 time.

6 Café Fresa y Chocolate

It doesn't look much from the outside, but **Café Fresa y Chocolate** (Calle 23, btwn Calles 10 & 12; ⊘9am-11pm), next to the Cuban film institute, is where young film aficionados go to dissect Almodóvar and Gutiérrez Alea. Grab a *cerveza* and join the discussion.

7 Café Cantante Mi Habana

Café Cantante Mi Habana (🖉7-879-0710; cnr Paseo & Calle 39; ⊘8pm-3am) is known as the best after-dark place to meet cool, fashion-conscious Cubans. This crowded but 'open' live-music and dancing venue inside the Teatro Nacional has recently garnered a reputation for its Saturday night gay parties.

A B C D

1

For reviews see

Straits of Florida

Malecón

Calzada

Línea

Paseo

Malecón

Calzada

Línea

Parque Lennon

Av 5

Río Almendares

Av 3

Río Almendares

Av 31

Av 41

Av 29

C 49C

Calz de Zapata

Necrópolis Cristóbal Colón

San Antonio Chiquito

NUEVO VEDADO

La Torre

Protestantes

E

F

G

H

US Embassy ● Plaza Tribuna
Anti-Imperialista

Calzada

Monumento a las
Víctimas del Maine

9 ◉

C J
C K
C L

Edificio
Focsa

31 ◉

2 ◉
Hotel
Nacional

Malecón (Av de Maceo)

0   500 m
0   0.25 miles

1

Calzada

C 3   C 9   C J
C H

Av de los
Presidentes

6 ◉

10 ◉

Museo de
Danza

C G (Av de los Presidentes)

21 ◉

19 ◉

Línea

C 15
C 17
C 19
C 21
C 25

17 ◉   24 ◉

7 ◉   12 ◉

34 🅐   C 23   22 ◉

C N

29 ◉

8 ◉
Habana
Libre   C 27

Av Universidad

26 ◉

Hospital
Príncipe
Vapor
Jovellar
San Lázaro

Calz de la Infanta

Espada

C O
C P

C M
C L

2

4 ◉
Museo de
Artes
Decorativas

C F
C E

15 ◉

Universidad
de la Habana

5 ◉

1 ◉
Museo
Napoleónico

San Martín

San Francisco
San Miguel
San Rafael
Neptuno
Concordia

Espada
Hospital
Aramburu
San Miguel

Soledad
Oquendo

Zanja

C 23

C 25
C 27
CD
CC
CB

CA

13 ◉

Av Universidad

Calz de Zapata

Calz de Zapata

Quinta de los
Molinos

11 ◉   Av Salvador Allende

Salud

Pocito

3

Paseo

C 31
C 33
C 35
C 37

Paseo

Calz de Zapata

33 ◉

Av de Carlos de Máde Céspedes

Av de la Independencia

Pozos Dulces

C 19 de Mayo

Bruzón

Luaces

Sitio

Desagüe

Enrique Barnet

Maloja

Retiro

Árbol Seco

Santo Tómas

Benjumeda

Clavel

Oquendo

4

Protestantes

C 39

Bellavista

Panorama

Av de Colón

Plaza de la
Revolución

3 ◉
Memorial a
José Martí

Aeropuerto
Internacional
José Martí
✈ (25km)

Aranguren

Arroyo (Av Manglar)

Calz de Ayestarán

Av 20 de Mayo

Calz de la Infanta

5

Sights

Museo Napoleónico MUSEUM

1 ◎ Map p72, G3

Without a doubt one of the best museums in Havana and, by definition, Cuba, this magnificently laid-out collection of 7000 objects associated with the life of Napoleon Bonaparte was amassed by Cuban sugar baron Julio Lobo and politician Orestes Ferrara. (San Miguel No 1159; CUC$3; ⊗9:30am-5pm Tue-Sat, 9:30am-12:30pm Sun)

Hotel Nacional HISTORIC BUILDING

2 ◎ Map p72, G1

Built in 1930 as a copy of the Breakers Hotel in Palm Beach, Florida, the eclectic art deco–neoclassical Hotel Nacional is a national monument and one of Havana's architectural emblems. (cnr Calles O & 21; ⊗free tours 10am & 3pm Mon-Fri, 10am Sat)

Local Life
City Bike Tours

CubaRuta Bikes (Map p72, C4; ☎52-47-66-33; www.cubarutabikes.com; Calle 16 No 152; city tour CUC$29) was Havana's first decent bicycle-hire and tour company when it started in 2013. Its guided cycling tours have proved to be consistently popular, particularly the three-hour classic city tour, which takes in the Bosque de la Habana, Plaza Vieja, Plaza de la Revolución, the Malecón and more. Book via phone or email at least a day in advance.

Memorial a José Martí MONUMENT

3 ◎ Map p72, F5

Center stage in Plaza de la Revolución is this monument, which at 138.5m is Havana's tallest structure. Fronted by an impressive 17m marble statue of a seated Martí in a pensive *Thinker* pose, the memorial houses a museum (the definitive word on Martí in Cuba) and a 129m lookout reached via a small CUC$2 lift (broken at last visit) with fantastic city views. (Plaza de la Revolución; CUC$3; ⊗9:30am-4pm Mon-Sat)

Museo de Artes Decorativas MUSEUM

4 ◎ Map p72, E2

One of Havana's best museums is something of a lost treasure half-hidden in the Vedado neighborhood. The decorative arts museum is replete with fancy rococo, Asian and art deco baubles. Equally interesting is the building itself, which is of French design and commissioned in 1924 by the wealthy Gómez family who built the Manzana de Gómez shopping center in Centro Habana. (Calle 17 No 502, btwn Calles D & E; CUC$3; ⊗9:30am-4pm Tue-Sat)

Universidad de la Habana UNIVERSITY

5 ◎ Map p72, G2

Founded by Dominican monks in 1728 and secularized in 1842, Havana University began life in Habana Vieja before moving to its present site in 1902. The existing neoclassical com-

Hotel Nacional (p74)

plex dates from the second quarter of the 20th century, and today some 30,000 students take courses here in social sciences, humanities, natural sciences, mathematics and economics. (cnr Calles L & San Lázaro)

Av de los Presidentes MONUMENT

6 ◉ Map p72, E2

Statues of illustrious Latin American leaders line the Las Ramblas–style Calle G (officially known as Av de los Presidentes), including Salvador Allende (Chile), Benito Juárez (Mexico) and Simón Bolívar. At the top of the avenue is a huge marble **Monumento a José Miguel Gómez** (Av de los Presidentes), Cuba's second president. At the other

end, the monument to his predecessor – Cuba's first president – Tomás Estrada Palma (long considered a US puppet) has been toppled, with just his shoes remaining on the original plinth.

Edificio Focsa LANDMARK

7 ◉ Map p72, F1

Unmissable on the Havana skyline, the modernist Edificio Focsa was built between 1954 and 1956 in a record 28 months using pioneering computer technology. In 1999 it was listed as one of the seven modern engineering wonders of Cuba. With 39 floors housing 373 apartments, it was, on its completion in June 1956, the second-largest concrete structure of its type in the world, built entirely without the use of cranes. (Focsa Bldg; cnr Calles 17 & M)

Hotel Habana Libre

NOTABLE BUILDING

8 ◎ Map p72, G2

This classic modernist hotel – the former Havana Hilton – was commandeered by Castro's revolutionaries in 1959 just nine months after it had opened, and was promptly renamed the Habana Libre. During the first few months of the revolution, Fidel ruled the country from a luxurious suite on the 24th floor. (Calle L, btwn Calles 23 & 25)

Monumento a las Víctimas del Maine

MONUMENT

9 ◎ Map p72, F1

West beyond the Hotel Nacional is a monument (1926) to the 266

American marines who were killed when the battleship USS *Maine* blew up mysteriously in Havana harbor in 1898. The American eagle that once sat on top was decapitated during the 1959 revolution. (Malecón)

Museo de Danza

MUSEUM

10 ◎ Map p72, E2

A dance museum in Cuba – well, there's no surprise there. This well-laid-out exhibition space in an eclectic Vedado mansion collects objects from Cuba's rich dance history, with many artifacts drawn from the collection of ex-ballerina Alicia Alonso. (Línea No 365, cnr Av de los Presidentes; CUC$2; ◷10am-6pm Mon-Sat)

Quinta de los Molinos

GARDENS, LANDMARK

11 ◎ Map p72, G3

The former stately residence of Independence War general Máximo Gómez, the Quinta sits amid lush grounds that have been managed as botanical gardens since 1839. While the former Gómez residence is currently closed, the grounds have recently reopened as a botanical garden with 160 tree species, 40 bird species and the tiny colorful polymita snails that are endemic to Cuba. There's also a butterfly enclosure, the first of its type in the country. Guided visits only. (cnr Av Salvador Allende & Luaces; guided tour CUC$5; ◷by tour 10am Tue & Sat)

Local Life

Plaza de la Revolución

Conceived by French urbanist Jean Claude Forestier in the 1920s, the gigantic **Plaza de la Revolución** (Map p72, F4), known as Plaza Cívica until 1959, was part of Havana's 'new city,' which grew up between 1920 and 1959. As the nexus of Forestier's ambitious plan, the square was built on a small hill (the Loma de los Catalanes) in the manner of Paris' Place de l'Étoile, with various avenues fanning out toward the Río Almendares, Vedado and the Parque de la Fraternidad in Centro Habana.

Eating

Café Laurent INTERNATIONAL $$

12 🍴 Map p72, F2

Talk about a hidden gem. The unsigned Café Laurent is a sophisticated fine-dining restaurant encased, incongruously, in a glaringly ugly 1950s apartment block next to the Focsa Building. Starched white tablecloths, polished glasses and lacy drapes furnish the bright modernist interior, while sautéed pork with dry fruit and red wine, and seafood risotto headline the menu. (🕿7-832-6890; Calle M No 257, 5th fl, btwn Calles 19 & 21; meals CUC$10-15; ⊙noon-midnight)

Starbien INTERNATIONAL $$

13 🍴 Map p72, E3

The ingredients: an elegant tucked-away Vedado mansion, an authentic Cuban welcome, complimentary bites to start you off, a great wine list, never-miss-a-beat service, and chicken in pineapple sauce. And it's all yours for CUC$12 if you bag the lunchtime special four-course menu. So get over to Calle 29 near Plaza de la Revolución. (🕿7-830-0711; Calle 29 No 205, btwn Calles B & C; lunch CUC$12; ⊙noon-5pm & 7pm-midnight)

Atelier CUBAN $$$

14 🍴 Map p72, C2

The first thing that hits you here is the stupendous wall art – huge, thought-provoking, religious-tinged paintings. You'll also notice the antique wooden ceiling, Moorish-style roof terrace and

old-school elegance (even the plates are interesting). At some point you'll get around to the food – Cuban with a French influence – scribbled onto an ever-changing menu. Try the duck (the specialty) if it's on, or the rabbit. (🕿7-836-2025; Calle 5 No 511/Altos, btwn Paseo & Calle 2; meals CUC$12-25; ⊙noon-midnight)

Café Presidente INTERNATIONAL $

15 🍴 Map p72, F3

With its red awnings and huge glass windows doing a good impersonation of a Champs-Élysées bistro, the Presidente delivers the goods on Havana's very own Champs-Élysées, Av de los Presidentes. It's the kind of place where you won't feel awkward popping in for a quick milk shake or plate of pasta, but it also does killer breakfasts and coffee. (🕿7-832-3091; cnr Av de los Presidentes & Calle 25; breakfast CUC$4-6.50; ⊙9am-midnight)

Decameron
INTERNATIONAL $$$

16 ⊗ Map p72, D2

Nondescript from the outside, but far prettier within, thanks largely to its famous collection of antique clocks (don't be late now!), the Decameron is an old stalwart paladar that was always good, still is good and probably always will be good. The food is Cuban with international inflections. People rave about the savory tuna tart; ditto the sweet lemon tart. (📞7-832-2444; Linea No 753, btwn Paseo & Calle 2; mains CUC$12-18; ⊗noon-midnight; ⊘)

Le Chansonnier
FRENCH $$$

17 ⊗ Map p72, F2

A great place to dine if you can find it (there's no sign), hidden away in a faded mansion turned private restaurant whose revamped interior is dramatically more modern than the front facade. French wine and French flavors shine in house specialties such as rabbit with mustard, eggplant gratin and spare ribs. Opening times vary and it's often busy; phone ahead. (📞7-832-1576; www.lechansonnierhabana. com; Calle J No 257, btwn Calles 13 & 15; meals CUC$12-20; ⊗12:30pm-12:30am)

Versus 1900
INTERNATIONAL $$$

18 ⊗ Map p72, D2

Opened in late 2015, Versus 1900 shows how Cuban restaurants are moving the yardstick ever forward. Set inside a large detached house and making good use of the multifarious space including interior rooms, front

SISOJE/ISTOCK/GETTY IMAGES ©

Restaurant in Vedado

terrace and rooftop, the place is exquisitely decorated (antique, but uncluttered) and delivers an interesting menu that includes rabbit, duck and Peruvian soup. (☑7-835-1852; www.versus1900.com; Línea No 504, btwn Calles D & E; mains CUC$7-24; ☉noon-midnight)

El Idilio
CUBAN $$

19 Map p72, E2

A bold, adventurous, neighborhood joint in Vedado with checkered tablecloths, Idilio epitomizes the Cuban culinary scene as it spreads its wings and flies. Anything goes here: pasta, ceviche and Cuban standards, or opt for the seafood medley peeled freshly off the barbecue before your very eyes. (☑7-830-7921; cnr Av de los Presidentes & Calle 15; meals CUC$6-11; ☉noon-midnight)

La Chucheria
AMERICAN $

20 Map p72, D1

Clinging to its perch close to the Malecón, this sleek sports bar looks as if it floated mockingly across the straits from Florida like a returning exile. But you can forget about politics momentarily as you contemplate pizza toppings, sandwich fillings and the best ice cream and fruit milk shakes in Havana. (Calle 1, btwn Calles C & D; snacks CUC$2-7; ☉7am-midnight)

La Torre
FRENCH, CARIBBEAN $$$

Havana's tallest restaurant is perched high above Vedado on the 36th floor of the skyline-hogging Focsa building

(see 7 Map p72, F1). The lofty fine-dining extravaganza has sweeping city views that rarely disappoint, although the food sometimes does. (☑7-838-3088; Edificio Focsa, cnr Calles 17 & M; mains CUC$15-30; ☉11:30am-12:30am)

Mediterraneo Havana
MEDITERRANEAN $$

21 Map p72, E2

Allying themselves with the *granja a la mesa* (farm-to-table) movement and utilizing a couple of agricultural co-ops in Guanabacoa, the Med serves primarily Italian food with a few nods to Spain in a pleasant Vedado residence. Run by two Cuban-Sardinian friends, it hits most of the right notes, with pasta dishes that aren't afraid to go out of the box. (☑7-832-4894; www.medhavana.com; Calle 13 No 406, btwn Calles F & G; mains CUC$9-18; ☉noon-midnight)

Local Life
LGBT Vedado

The focus of Havana's gay life is centered on a 'triangle' of streets in western Vedado. The intersection of Calle 23 and the Malecón has long been a favored meeting spot for gay people, while Cine Yara and the Coppelia park opposite are well-known cruising spots. There are also several gay-friendly nightclubs in the vicinity hosting drag shows.

For dinner, try **Toke Infanta y 25** (Map p72, G2; ☎7-836-3440; cnr Calzada de la Infanta & Calle 25; snacks CUC$2-4; ⏰7am-midnight), which has become known as a gay-friendly spot lately due to its location next to a couple of nightclubs. Sitting pretty amid the bruised edifices of Calzada de la Infanta on the cusp of Vedado and Centro Habana, it lures enamored *habaneros* (and tourists) with cool neon, smart color accents, economical *hamburguesas* (hamburgers) and chocolate brownies.

Waoo Snack Bar INTERNATIONAL $

22 ✖ Map p72, G2

Wow! The Waoo Snack Bar truly impresses with its wooden wraparound bar, happening location close to Calles 23 and L, and quick offerings you might want to savor – think carpaccio, cheese plates and coffee with accompanying desserts. (Calle L No 414, cnr Calle 25; snacks CUC$3-7; ⏰noon-midnight)

Drinking

Café Madrigal BAR

23 🍷 Map p72, D3

Vedado flirts with bohemia in this dimly lit romantic bar that might have materialized serendipitously from Paris' Latin Quarter in the days of Joyce and Hemingway. Order a *tapita* (small tapa) and a cocktail, and retire to the atmospheric art nouveau terrace where the buzz of nighttime conversation competes with the racket of vintage American cars rattling past below. (Calle 17 No 302, btwn Calles 2 & 4; ⏰6pm-2am Tue-Sun)

Café Mamainé CAFE, BAR

24 🍷 Map p72, F1

Art and coffee go together like Fidel and Che in this wonderfully reimagined eclectic mansion with an interior decked out with revolving local art, much of it made from recycled 'junk.' Flop down on a cushion on the wooden mezzanine, order a strong coffee or cocktail and chat with the person next to you (probably an artist). (☎7-832-8328; Calle L No 206, btwn Calles 15 & 17; ⏰8am-midnight Mon-Thu, 8am-3am Fri-Sun)

Bar-Restaurante 1830 CLUB

25 🍷 Map p72, B3

If you want to salsa dance, this is *the* place to go. After the Sunday night show literally everyone takes to the floor. It's at the far west end of the Malecón with a water-facing terrace.

Skip the food. (cnr Malecón & Calle 20; ☺noon-1:45am)

Cabaret Las Vegas CLUB

26 🔇 Map p72, G2

The Vegas was once a rough and slightly seedy local music dive, but these days it's better known for its late-night drag shows. With the demise of Humboldt 25, it's become one of Havana's most reliable gay clubs. (Calzada de la Infanta No 104, btwn Calles 25 & 27; entry CUC$5; ☺10pm-4am)

Chill Out BAR

Chill Out doesn't need much more explanation beyond its name. It's the

trance-y, super-cool rooftop bar at Versus 1900 (see 18 🔇 Map p72, D2), with sofas, poufs and four-poster recliners. The ideal after-party haunt in Vedado. (Línea No 504, btwn Calles D & E; ☺7pm-3am)

Piano Bar Delirio Habanero CLUB

This sometimes suave, sometimes frenetic lounge upstairs in Teatro Nacional de Cuba (see 33 ✪ Map p72, F4) hosts everything from young rap artists to smooth, improvised jazz. The sharp red-accented bar and performance space abut a wall of glass overlooking Plaza de la Revolución – it's impressive

PHIL CLARKE HILL/GETTY IMAGES©

Jazz Club la Zorra y El Cuervo (p83)

Understand

Forestier & the Beautification of Havana

Paris and Havana share at least one thing in common aside from the Panthéon-mimicking Capitolio building – landscape architect Jean-Claude Nicolas Forestier.

Fresh from high-profile commissions in the French capital, Forestier arrived in Havana in 1925 to draw up a master-plan to link the city's fast-growing urban grid. The landscaper – a strong advocate of the 'city beautiful' movement – spent the next five years sketching broad tree-lined boulevards, Parisian-style squares and a harmonious city landscape designed to accentuate Havana's iconic monuments and lush tropical setting.

Central to the plan was a civic center (to be called Plaza de la República) located on the Loma de Catalanes, a hill that stood at the southern edge of Vedado, from which a series of avenues would radiate outwards in the manner of Paris' Place de l'Étoile. Forestier envisaged that the civic center would be embellished with fountains and gardens and anchored by a huge memorial to José Martí. To the west, the space would link to a grand network of parks that followed the course of the Río Almendares.

The onset of the Great Depression coupled with political unrest in Cuba in the 1930s put the brakes on many of Forestier's plans, although a few of his ideas were adopted before his death in 1930. These included the lush Av del Puerto by the harbor, the famous staircase in front of the university and the reimagining of the 'Prado.'

It took another 25 years before the Frenchman's Parisian vision for Havana was finally realized, with vast construction projects enacted in the 1950s. The civic center ultimately became Plaza de la Revolución, with its grand Martí Memorial, while the wide avenues were built as Paseo and Av de los Presidentes (Calle G), both adorned with tree-lined central walkways and heroic busts and statues.

Forestier is sometimes seen as Havana's Baron Haussmann (the civic planner who redesigned Paris in the 1860s), but unlike Haussmann, who tore down much of medieval Paris, Forestier was adamant about not disturbing the city's old quarter, Habana Vieja. For that we have much to thank him for.

at night with the Martí memorial alluringly backlit. (📞7-878-4275; cnr Paseo & Calle 39; cover charge CUC$5-$10.; ⊘from 6pm Tue-Sun)

Entertainment

Cabaret Parisién   CABARET

One rung down from Marianao's world-famous Tropicana, but cheaper and closer to the city center, the nightly Cabaret Parisién in the Hotel Nacional (see 2 🔵 Map p72, G1) is well worth a look, especially if you're staying in or around Vedado. It's the usual mix of frills, feathers and semi-naked women (and men), but the choreography is first class and the costumes wonderfully flamboyant. (📞7-836-3564; Hotel Nacional, cnr Calles 21 & O; entry CUC$35; ⊘9pm)

Fábrica de Arte Cubano   LIVE PERFORMANCE

27 ⭐ Map p72, B4

The brainchild of Afro-Cuban fusion musician X-Alfonso, this is one of Havana's finest new art projects. An intellectual nexus for live music, art expos, fashion shows and invigorating debate over coffee and cocktails, there isn't a pecking order or surly bouncer in this converted cooking-oil factory in Vedado. (📞7-838-2260; www.fabricadeartecubano.com; cnr Calle 26 & 11; CUC$2; ⊘8pm-3am Thu-Sun)

Centro Cultural El Gran Palenque   DANCE

28 ⭐ Map p72, C2

Founded in 1962, the high-energy Conjunto Folklórico Nacional de Cuba specializes in Afro-Cuban dancing (all of the drummers are Santería priests). See them perform here, and dance along during the regular Sábado de Rumba – three full hours of mesmerizing drumming and dancing. This group also performs at Teatro Mella and internationally. (Calle 4 No 103, btwn Calzada & Calle 5; CUC$5; ⊘3-6pm Sat)

Jazz Café   LIVE MUSIC

This upscale joint, located improbably in the Galerías de Paseo shopping mall (see 35 🔒 Map p72, C2) overlooking the Malecón, is a kind of jazz supper club, with dinner tables and a decent menu. At night, the club swings into action with live jazz, *timba* and, occasionally, straight-up salsa. It's definitely the suavest of Havana's jazz venues. (📞7-838-3302; top fl, Galerías de Paseo, cnr Calle 1 & Paseo; cover after 8pm CUC$10; ⊘noon-2am)

Jazz Club la Zorra y El Cuervo   LIVE MUSIC

29 ⭐ Map p72, G2

Havana's most famous jazz club (The Vixen and the Crow) opens its doors nightly at 10pm to long lines of committed music fiends. Enter through a red

Fábrica de Arte Cubano (p83)

British phonebox and descend into a diminutive and dark basement. The scene here is hot and clamorous and leans toward freestyle jazz. (📞7-833-2402; cnr Calles 23 & O; CUC$5-10; ⏰from 10pm)

Casa de las Américas
LIVE PERFORMANCE

30 ⭐ Map p72, D1

A powerhouse of Cuban and Latin American culture set up by Moncada survivor Haydee Santamaría in 1959, offering conferences, exhibitions, a gallery, a bookstore, concerts and an atmosphere of erudite intellectualism. The Casa's annual literary award is one of the Spanish-speaking world's most prestigious. See the website for the schedule of upcoming events. (📞7-838-2706; www.casa.co.cu; cnr Calles 3 & G)

El Gato Tuerto
LIVE MUSIC

31 ⭐ Map p72, G1

Once the headquarters of Havana's alternative artistic and sexual scene, the 'one-eyed cat' is now a nexus for middle-aged karaoke singers who come here to knock out rum-fueled renditions of traditional Cuban boleros (ballads). It's hidden just off the Malecón in a quirky two-story house with turtles swimming in a front pool. (Calle O No 14, btwn Calles 17 & 19; drink minimum CUC$5; ⏰noon-6am)

Habana Café CABARET

32 ⭐ Map p72, C2

A hip and trendy nightclub-cum-cabaret-show at the Hotel Meliá Cohiba laid out in 1950s American style, but with salsa music. After 1am the tables are cleared and the place rocks to 'international music' until the cock crows. Excellent value. (Paseo, btwn Calles 1 & 3; CUC$20; ⏲from 9pm)

Teatro Nacional de Cuba THEATER

33 ⭐ Map p72, F4

One of the twin pillars of Havana's cultural life, the Teatro Nacional de Cuba on Plaza de la Revolución is the modern rival to the Gran Teatro in Centro Habana. Built in the 1950s as part of Jean Forestier's grand city expansion, the complex hosts landmark concerts, foreign theater troupes and La Colmenita children's company. (📞7-879-6011; cnr Paseo & Calle 39; per person CUC$10; ⏲box office 10am-5pm & before performances)

Shopping

Bazar Estaciones GIFTS & SOUVENIRS

34 🔒 Map p72, F2

This is a new lovingly curated private shop selling some interesting and unique souvenirs (not the standard government-branded stuff). It's on the upper floor of a Vedado mansion right on the main drag. (📞7-832-9965; Calle 23 No 10, btwn Calles J & I; ⏲10am-9pm)

Galerías de Paseo SHOPPING CENTER

35 🔒 Map p72, C2

Across the street from the Hotel Meliá Cohiba, this supposedly upscale shopping center was getting an overdue upgrade at the time of research. It sells well-made clothes and other consumer items to tourists and affluent Cubans, and also hosts the peerless Jazz Café (p83). (cnr Calle 1 & Paseo; ⏲9am-6pm Mon-Sat, to 1pm Sun)

◯ Local Life
Cuba Libro

Cafe, book vendor, socially responsible community resource, and a great place for Cubans and non-Cubans to interact; **Cuba Libro** (Map p72, B4; 📞7-830-5205; cnr Calles 24 & 19; ⏲11am-8pm Mon-Sat; 🚻) wears many different hats. Although it's a bit of a walk from the main sights, this wonderfully tranquil little nook is a good place to find out more about Havana below the radar. Grab a juice or coffee and join the discussion.

Explore

Playa & Marianao

Playa, west of Vedado across the Río Almendares, is a large, complex municipality anchored by Miramar, a leafy diplomatic quarter of broad avenues, weeping laurel trees and fine private restaurants. Further west lies Cubanacán with its scientific fairs and biotechnological and pharmaceutical research institutes; the street-art extravaganza of Fusterlandia; and the slightly edgier residential neighborhood of Marianao.

THE VISUAL EXPLORER/SHUTTERSTOCK ©

The Sights in a Day

☀ Start off in the tree-lined diplomatic quarter of Miramar. The neighborhood doesn't get going particularly early so kill an hour strolling through **Parque Almendares** (p90), a shady haven that ought to extinguish any Vedado-acquired hangovers. Next, head down Quinta Avenida (Av 5), Miramar's main drag, admiring **La Casa de las Tejas Verdes** (p93) and perhaps stopping off at **Casa del Habano Quinta** (p97) to buy some cigars.

☀ You're spoiled for lunch in Playa and it gets no better than the food hot off the grill at **La Fontana** (p91). Relax afterward with a coffee at **Café Fortuna Joe** (p91) before trekking west breaking the journey at the **Fundación Naturaleza y El Hombre** (p93) and the resplendent **Iglesia Jesús de Miramar** (p91). The highlight of the day comes at **Fusterlandia** (p88), the psychedelic art neighborhood that literally brims with mosaics.

☾ In the evening double back west for tapas and cocktails at ultra-trendy **Espacios** (p91) before claiming your pre-booked ticket at the unashamedly kitschy bulwark of Havana's after-dark scene, the **Tropicana Nightclub** (p96; pictured left).

For a local's day in Playa, see p90.

👁 **Top Sights**

Fusterlandia (p88)

🔍 **Local Life**

Unsignposted Playa (p90)

💜 **Best of Havana**

Eating
La Fontana (p91)

El Aljibe (p94)

La Corte del Príncipe (p95)

Art & Architecture
Fusterlandia (p88)

Espacios (p91)

Iglesia Jesús de Miramar (p91)

Live Music
Casa de la Música (p97)

Salón Rosado Benny Moré (p91)

Café Miramar (p96)

Getting There & Away

🚌 **Bus** The best way to get to Playa from Centro Habana and Vedado is on the Habana Bus Tour T1, which plies most of the neighborhood's highlights (CUC$10 for an all-day ticket). Plenty of metro buses also make the trip; P-1 and P-10 buses are the most useful.

Top Sights
Fusterlandia

Where does art go after Gaudí? For a hint, head west from central Havana to the seemingly low-key district of Jaimanitas, where Cuban artist José Fuster has turned his home neighborhood into a masterpiece of intricate tilework and kaleidoscopic colors – a street-art extravaganza. Imagine Gaudí on steroids relocated to a tropical setting.

👁 Map p92, B4

cnr Calle 226 & Av 3

admission free

Neighborhood Sign

Welcoming you to the Fusterlandia 'show' is the Jaimanitas neighborhood sign etched with the words 'Homenaje a Gaudí' (Homage to Gaudí) arranged in a vivid mosaic. Branching out from here, Fuster's surrealistic ceramics cover several city blocks, encompassing park benches, public spaces and over 80 local houses. Bus stops, street signs and even a doctor's surgery have all had an artistic makeover.

Taller-Estudio José Fuster

The centerpiece of the project is Fuster's own house. **Taller-Estudio José Fuster** (cnr Calle 226 & Av 3; admission free; ⏰9am-4pm Wed-Sun) is a multi-level residence decorated from roof to foundations by art, sculpture and – above all – mosaic tiles of every color and description. The overall impression defies written description (just GO!), a fantastical mishmash of spiraling walkways, giant hands, cowboys with Picasso-esque faces and sunburst fountains centered around a small pool. The work mixes homages to Picasso and Gaudí with snippets of Gauguin and Wifredo Lam, elements of magic realism, strong maritime influences, and a cap doffed to Santería.

The Bus Stops

There's no mistaking Fusterlandia's disembarkation point for visitors arriving by bus. Two local bus stops on either side of Quinta Avenida (Av 5) have been given the full Fuster treatment with decorative curves, toadstool-like roofs and the stop name and number picked out in mosaic tiles.

MEGAPRESS/ALAMY ©

☑ Top Tips

▶ You can buy art at numerous workshops set up around the neighborhood, including Fuster's own studio.

▶ For the best view of Fusterlandia climb up the observation tower inside Fuster's house.

▶ Reserve time to stroll around the quieter streets of the neighborhood and meet some of its residents.

✗ Take a Break

Jaimanitas has recently sprouted a pretty good restaurant decorated, not surprisingly, with cutting-edge art. **El Cucalambe** (Map p92, B4; Calle 226; mains CUC$5-9; ⏰noon-11pm) is named for an erstwhile Las Tunas poet and has tables set around a pleasant outdoor patio. Otherwise, you'll have to stroll 1km west to Marina Hemingway to grab a pizza in **Restaurante la Cova** (Map p92, A4; ☎7-209-7289; cnr Av 5 & Calle 248; meals CUC$8; ⏰noon-midnight).

Local Life
Unsignposted Playa

Playa doesn't always advertise its best bits. Call it confidence, arrogance, negligence or whatever, but the neighborhood guards a rich raft of secrets that are worth seeking out.

❶ Parque Almendares

First things first – this is no manicured European park with gravel walkways and shapely shrubs and you won't find many tourists here, but, as an ecological revitalization project **Parque Almendares** is impressive and important. It's also a sacred Santería site where adherents often leave ritual offerings beneath trees. Stroll along the riverside under the green canopy and peruse the unusual sights.

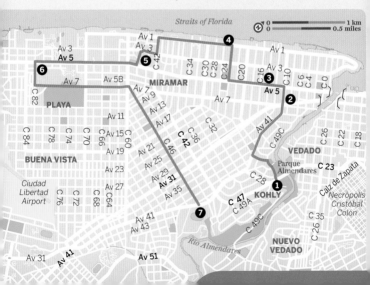

2 Espacios

When the *au courant* tapas-bar-cum-chill-out lounge of **Espacios** (☑7-202-2921; Calle 10 No 513, btwn Avs 5 & 7; tapas CUC$3-6; ☺noon-6am) opened a few years ago, it built up its reputation by word of mouth. There's no sign outside the large detached house it inhabits in Miramar. Instead, you have to know someone hip enough to have been there to find out the address.

3 Quinta Avenida

Before the revolution, Miramar was a posh residential quarter where Cuba's richest people lived in huge ostentatious mansions. When many residents fled to the US in the 1960s, their properties were requisitioned by the Cuban government and turned into embassies and offices. Today, arterial Quinta Avenida retains a dizzying cavalcade of fine eclectic architecture.

4 Café Fortuna Joe

There are two Café Fortunas in Miramar, both of them pretty outlandish, but only **one** (☑54-13-37-06; cnr Calle 24 & Av 1, Miramar; ☺9am-midnight) has the suffix 'Joe.' The Fortuna in question is perched above a restaurant called El Palio on Av 1. Inside you can enjoy some of Havana's best coffee in some of its weirdest seating booths, including a horse carriage, a boat and even a toilet!

5 La Fontana

Finding Havana's finest grill-restaurant has always been a bit of an Easter-egg hunt. It's tucked away behind high walls in a tangled section of Miramar's road grid. But, once inside **La Fontana** (☑7-202-8337; www.lafontanahavana.info; Av 3a No 305; mains CUC$20-28; ☺noon-midnight), it's like the hungry 1990s never happened, with giant steaks, ceviche and a super-cool chill-out lounge on offer.

6 Iglesia Jesús de Miramar

Miramar's **church** (Map p92; cnr Av 5 & Calle 82; ☺9am-noon & 4-6pm) doesn't feature much in Havana's potted sights. It's considered too modern, too peripheral and too ordinary by people who've never been here. But the church's true glory lies within: 14 giant 'stations of the cross' painted in resplendent detail across the walls. You'll see nothing like it anywhere else in Cuba.

7 Salón Rosado Benny Moré

Often considered too *caliente* (hot) for 'wimpy' outsiders, **Salón Rosado Benny Moré** (El Tropical; ☑7-206-1281; cnr Av 41 & Calle 46, Kohly; ☺9pm-late), or El Tropical as it's colloquially known, is a live-music stronghold favored by the mainly young and the mainly local. While tourists fork out CUC$75-plus to attend the nearby Tropicana cabaret, Cubans pay CUC$1 to enter El Tropical and see top salsa acts in a more jam-packed, slightly more basic outdoor setting.

Straits of Florida

Caleta de San Lázaro

VEDADO

C 28
C 26
C 23
C 35
C 10
C 6
La Casa de las
Tejas Verdes
C 16
C 20
C 24
C 28
C 30
C 34
Parque
Miramar
C 32
C 36
C 42
C 490
Parque
Almendares
C 28
**NUEVO
VEDADO**
C 26
Av Kohly
KOHLY
C 490
C 47
C 490
Av 51
Río Almendares

Av 1
Av 3
Av 5
Av 7
Av 1
Av 3
Av 5
Av 7
Av 9
Av 11
Av 13
Av 17
Av 41
Av 31
Av 33
Av 35
Av 37
Av 29
Av 25
Av 21
Av 41
Av 43
Av 51
Av 41

MIRAMAR

Acuario
Nacional

La Maqueta
de la Capital

C 62
C 66
C 60
C 66
C 70
C 74
C 78
C 82
C 84
C 19
C 23
C 27
C 64
C 68
C 72
C 76

Fundación
Naturaleza y
El Hombre

Parque
Monte
Barreto

PLAYA

BUENA VISTA

Ciudad
Libertad
Airport

C 92
C 96
C 112
C 120

Circo
Trompoloco

Isla del
Coco

Río Quibú

Inset
(3km)

MARIANAO

Inset

JAIMANITAS

Fusterlandia
C 222
El Cucalambé
Río Jaimanitas

Caleta de
San Lázaro

Restaurante
la Cova
Av 1
C 248
Marina
Hemingway
Av 5

500 m
0.25 miles

1 km
0.5 miles

For reviews see	
◉ Top Sights	p88
◉ Sights	p93
✕ Eating	p94
✿ Entertainment	p96
🛍 Shopping	p97

3
6
10 ✕
16 ✕
4 ◉
12 ✕
9 ◉
1 ◉
2
8 ✕
14 ✿
15
13 ✿
5 ◉
7 ◉
11 ✿

Sights

Acuario Nacional
AQUARIUM

1 ⊙ Map p92, C1

Founded in 1960, the national aquarium is a Havana institution that gets legions of annual visitors. Despite its rather scruffy appearance, this place leaves most other Cuban *acuarios* (aquatic centers) in the shade (which isn't saying much). Saltwater fish are the specialty, but there are also sea lions and dolphins, including hourly dolphin shows. Note, however, that dolphin performances are widely criticized by animal welfare groups who claim the captivity of such complex marine mammals is debilitating and stressful for the animals. (🖉7-202-5872; cnr Av 3 & Calle 62; adult/child CUC\$10/7; ⊙10am-6pm Tue-Sun)

Fundación Naturaleza y El Hombre
MUSEUM

2 ⊙ Map p92, C2

This tiny museum seems to confirm the old adage that 'small is beautiful,' displaying artifacts from a 17,422km canoe trip from the Amazon source to the sea, led by Cuban intellectual and anthropologist António Núñez Jiménez in 1987. Exhibits in this astounding array of items include one of Cuba's largest photography collections, books written by the prolific Núñez Jiménez, his beloved canoe, and a famous portrait of Fidel by Ecuadorian painter Oswaldo Guayasamín. (🖉7-209-2885; Av 5b No 6611, btwn Calles 66 & 70; CUC\$2; ⊙8:30am-3pm Mon-Fri)

La Casa de las Tejas Verdes
HISTORIC BUILDING

3 ⊙ Map p92, E2

Emerging from the tunnel under the Río Almendares, your first glimpse of Miramar is the so-called 'house of the green tiles,' a subtle hint of the eclecticism to come: this is the only example of Queen Anne architecture in Cuba. The house was built in 1926, and, for most of its existence, was the home of a semifamous Havana socialite, Luisa Rodríguez Faxas, who lived here from 1943 to 1999. (🖉7-212-5282; Calle 2 No 308, btwn Avs 3 & 5; admission free; ⊙by appointment)

La Maqueta de la Capital
MUSEUM

4 ⊙ Map p92, D1

Havana itself is somewhat dilapidated in parts and so, ironically, is this huge 1:1000 scale model of the city that looks like it could do with a good dusting. The model was originally created for urban-planning purposes, but is now a tourist attraction. It is going through a protracted renovation, but can usually still be viewed. (Calle 28 No 113, btwn Avs 1 & 3; CUC\$3; ⊙9:30am-5pm Mon-Fri)

Marina Hemingway
MARINA

5 ⊙ Map p92, A4

Havana's premier marina was constructed in 1953 in the small coastal community of Santa Fé. After the revolution it was nationalized and named after Castro's favorite *Yanqui*. The marina has four 800m-long channels, a dive center, a motley collection of shops and restaurants, and two hotels (one currently disused), so it's only worth visiting if you're docking your boat or utilizing the water-sports facilities. (cnr Av 5 & Calle 248)

Eating

La Cocina de Lilliam
FUSION $$$

6 🍴 Map p92, C2

A legend long before Cuban food became legendary, Lilliam's was once one of Havana's only posh private

restaurants – the long-standing diplomat's choice. These days it has more competition, but maintains its prominence with classy service, secluded ambience and freshly cooked food to die for. (📞7-209-6514; www. lacocinadelilliam.com; Calle 48 No 1311, btwn Avs 13 & 15; meals CUC$15-30; ⏱noon-3pm & 7-11pm Tue-Sat)

El Aljibe
CARIBBEAN $$

7 🍴 Map p92, D2

On paper a humble state-run restaurant, but in reality a rip-roaring culinary extravaganza, El Aljibe has been delighting both Cuban and foreign diplomats' taste buds for years. The furore surrounds the gastronomic mysteries of just one dish: the obliga-

BERTRAND GARDEL/HEMIS/ALAMY ©

Restaurant at Marina Hemingway

tory *pollo asado* (roast chicken), which is served up with as-much-as-you-can-eat helpings of white rice, black beans, fried plantain, french fries and salad. (☑7-204-1583/4; Av 7, btwn Calles 24 & 26; mains CUC$12-15; ⊙noon-midnight)

La Corte del Príncipe   ITALIAN $$$

8 🍴 Map p92, C2

Possibly the most Italian of Italian restaurants in Havana is this lovely semi-alfresco nook run by an expat Italian who plies the best of his country's famous cuisine. The menu's a potluck inscribed on a blackboard, but there are regular appearances from eggplant parmigiano and *vitello tonnato* (veal in tuna sauce). Shiny fresh vegetables in display baskets add to the allure. (☑52-55-90-91; cnr Av 9 & Calle 74; mains CUC$15-20; ⊙noon-3pm & 7pm-midnight Tue-Sun)

La Casa del Gelato   ICE CREAM $

9 🍴 Map p92, C1

Miramar has always seemed to be one step ahead of the rest of Havana in the culinary stakes, sporting posh dining options when the rest of the city was still on iron rations. Now they've moved the goalposts again with this fabulous ice-cream parlor that smells of waffles, sells multiple flavors and even has a Nespresso coffee machine. (☑52-42-08-70; Av 1 No 4215, btwn Calles 42 & 44; ice cream CUC$2-4; ⊙11am-11pm)

La Esperanza   INTERNATIONAL $$$

10 🍴 Map p92, E1

The unassuming Esperanza was being gastronomically creative long before the 2011 reforms made life for chefs a lot easier. The interior of this vine-covered house is a riot of quirky antiques, old portraits and refined 1940s furnishings, while the food from the family kitchen includes such exquisite dishes as *pollo luna de miel* (chicken flambéed in rum) and lamb brochettes. (☑7-202-4361; Calle 16 No 105, btwn Avs 1 & 3; meals CUC$8-17; ⊙7-11pm Mon-Sat)

Paladar Vista Mar   SEAFOOD $$

11 🍴 Map p92, D1

The Vista Mar has been around for eons in paladar years (since 1996). It inhabits the 2nd-floor family room turned restaurant of a private residence, which faces the sea. The seaside ambience is embellished by a beautiful swimming pool that spills its water into the ocean. If enjoying delicious seafood dishes overlooking the crashing ocean sounds enticing, read no more, and book a table! (☎7-203-8328; www.restaurantevistamar.com; Av 1 No 2206, btwn Calles 22 & 24; mains CUC$8-15; ⏰noon-midnight Mon-Sat)

Cafetería Betty Boom   FAST FOOD $

Inhabiting the space once occupied by 'El Garage,' Betty Boom (see 1 Map p92, C1) offers a similar concept: cheap but good fast food (hot dogs, sandwiches, shakes and salads) in a retro 1950s diner interior where the waitresses dress like 1930s cartoon character Betty Boop. Opening hours are generous, as are the portions. There's a small outdoor terrace. (☎53-92-94-12; cnr Av 3 & Calle 60; snacks CUC$2.50-5; ⏰11am-2:30am)

✅ Top Tip

Salsa Dancing

Go into the woods at Parque Almendares to find one of Havana's most popular open-air discos, **El Salón Chévere** (☎52-64-96-92; cnr Calles 49 & 28; CUC$6-10; ⏰11pm-3am), where a healthy mix of Cubans and non-Cubans come to dance salsa. You can also take salsa lessons here through **Club Salseando Chévere** (www.salseando chevere.com; cnr Calles 49 & 28; per hour from CUC$25).

Club Su Miramar   KOREAN $$

12 ❌ Map p92, D1

Havana's restaurant scene in the last few years has been an exciting potluck of 'what's next?' We've already had Cuba's first Russian, Iranian and Indian restaurants. Now we have its first Korean place. You're halfway to Seoul in Club Su with the decor – a fragrant garden and tranquil terrace with sliding doors into an Asian-minimalist domain. The food's not far behind. (☎7-206-3443; Calle 40a No 1115, btwn Avs 1 & 3; mains CUC$9-14; ⏰noon-3am)

Entertainment

Tropicana Nightclub   CABARET

13 ⭐ Map p92, C4

A city institution since its 1939 opening, the world-famous Tropicana was one of the few bastions of Havana's Las Vegas–style nightlife to survive the revolution. Immortalized in Graham Greene's 1958 classic *Our Man in Havana,* the open-air cabaret show here has changed little since its 1950s heyday, with scantily clad *señoritas* descending from palm trees to dance Latin salsa amid bright lights. (☎7-267-1871; Calle 72 No 4504, Marianao; tickets from CUC$75; ⏰from 10pm)

Café Miramar   LIVE MUSIC

14 ⭐ Map p92, B2

Miramar's slick new jazz club wouldn't cut ice with bebop-era jazz greats who would smirk at the sanitized air and

Cigar store

no-smoking rule, but it doesn't seem to bother today's young innovators. The club is encased in the Cine Teatro Miramar and belongs to government agency ARTex. Things usually get jamming at 10pm-ish and there's cheap food. (Av 5 No 9401, cnr Calle 94; cover CUC$2)

Casa de la Música   LIVE MUSIC

15 ⭐ Map p92, E2

Launched with a concert by renowned jazz pianist Chucho Valdés in 1994, this Miramar favorite is run by national Cuban recording company Egrem, and the programs are generally a lot more authentic than the cabaret entertainment you'll see at the hotels.

(📞7-202-6147; Calle 20 No 3308, cnr Av 35, Miramar; CUC$5-20; ⏰from 10pm Tue-Sat)

Shopping

La Casa del
Habano Quinta   CIGARS

16 🔒 Map p92, E2

Arguably Havana's top cigar store – and there are many contenders. The primary reasons: it's well stocked, with well-informed staff, a comfy smoking lounge, a decent on-site restaurant and a welcome lack of tourist traffic. (📞7-214-4737; cnr Av 5 & Calle 16, Miramar; ⏰10am-6pm Mon-Sat, to 1pm Sun)

Explore

Habana del Este

Habana del Este is home to Playas del Este, a multiflavored if slightly unkempt beach strip situated 18km east of Habana Vieja. While the beaches here are sublime, the accompanying resorts aren't exactly luxurious. But for those who dislike modern beach development and prefer a more local scene, Playas del Este is a breath of fresh (sea) air.

The Sights in a Day

☀ In the morning visit the little fishing community of Cojímar, where you can immerse yourself in Hemingway nostalgia and admire the **Torreón de Cojímar** (p103; pictured left), a small fortification occupied briefly by the British in 1762. Stop for lunch in **Restaurante la Terraza** (p105), a one-time Hemingway haunt by the water.

☀ For something truly local, stop briefly in the proletarian neighborhood of **Alamar** (p103) where you can see one of Havana's largest farmer's markets and pop into one of its newest arts centers, **Centro Cultural Enguayabera** (p105). Hit the beaches in the afternoon. Which one depends on your personal taste. Playa Tarará offers **kiteboarding** (p103), El Megano is relatively quiet while Playa Santa María del Mar is party central in peak season.

🌙 Gravitate in the evening to the small beach town of Guanabo where you can hail a horse and cart to take you to **Il Piccolo** (p103), doyen of some of Havana's best pizza. For dessert, sample a potent dose of the local nightlife at **Bar Luna** (p105) or some other rocking beach shack.

For a local's day in Habana del Este, see p100.

🔍 Local Life

Havana's Eastern Beaches (p100)

♥ Best of Havana

Eating
Il Piccolo (p103)

Tours & Activities
Havana Kiteboarding Club (p103)

Getting There & Away

🚌 **Bus** Habana Bus Tour's T3 bus runs a service every 40 minutes from Parque Central to Playa Santa María del Mar. All-day tickets cost CUC$5. Bus A40 stops at the roundabout at Calle 462 and Av 5 in Guanabo before heading into Havana.

🚗 **Car** A taxi from Centro Habana to Playas del Este costs between CUC$15 and CUC$20

Local Life
Havana's Eastern Beaches

Havana's eastern beaches stretch for 15km in an almost unbroken line from Bacuranao in the west to Guanabo in the east. While none of the strip carries the tourist-heavy all-inclusive atmosphere of Varadero, each parcel of sand retains a distinct flavor, from gay-friendly Boca Ciega to the beach-town sensibilities of Guanabo. This is an ideal place to meet Cuban vacationers.

① Bacuranao
Bacuranao is the first decent beach heading east out of Havana, lying 12km from the city center. The small scoop of sand is a taste of things to come, but is separated from the strip further east by a rocky promontory. Bacuranao is largely a Cuban domain and sees few foreign visitors.

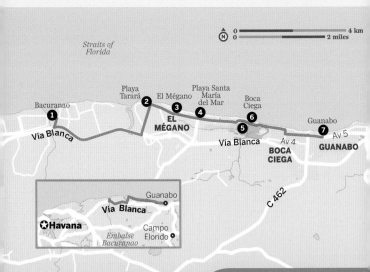

❷ Playa Tarará

The home of one of Havana's two marinas, **Tarará** supports its own resort village, a sprawling cluster of 1960s holiday bungalows still used mostly by Cuban vacationers. Plush it isn't, although the adjacent beach is pretty (if a little littered) and relatively quiet out of season. Known for its ocean whitecaps, the area has recently become a kiteboarding nexus.

❸ El Mégano

El Mégano, where the fun starts, is popular enough to justify its own *punto náutico* (renting out beach toys), but sufficiently detached to avoid the screaming reggaeton sometimes heard further east. If the crowds get too much, simply stroll further west toward Tarará and tranquility.

❹ Playa Santa María del Mar

Playas del Este's three main beach hotels line **Playa Santa María del Mar**, the high-quality stretch of sand protected by low dunes and shaded by occasional stands of palms. Various *punto náuticos* rent out beach kayaks, banana boats and other water toys.

❺ Laguna Itabo

A swampy lake surrounded by mangroves, this small lagoon sits just behind the dunes at the eastern end of Santa María del Mar. There's a hotel on its southern shore, but the best public access is through a little restaurant called Mi Cayito set on stilts above the water called. It's a popular spot with Cubans and a good place to see waterfowl.

❻ Boca Ciega

The dunes get higher as you approach **Boca Ciega**, a broad beach abutting a small river mouth and lagoon. Since the 1990s this has been known as Havana's unofficial gay beach. However, it's a low-key scene and, with the reopening of the nearby Hotel Arenal, you'll likely see as many straight couples as same-sex ones relaxing on sun-loungers.

❼ Guanabo

Backed by the small scruffy beach town of **Guanabo**, this eastern stretch of beach is a little stonier and not as well maintained as the others. The bonus is the lively town that abuts it. While there's no fancy promenade here, you'll encounter local life aplenty vibrating in an array of Cuban shops, bars and restaurants. Learn some Spanish and dive in.

For reviews see
- Sights p103
- Eating p103
- Drinking p105
- Entertainment p105

Straits of Florida

Av 5

C 506

C 502
C 500
Av 5C
Av 7
Av 9
C 488

GUANABO
Bvd Habana
C 482
Av 5
Av 7B
C 476

Playa
Guanabo
C 472
Av 7
Av 11
Av 13
C 464

BOCA
CIEGA
C 462
C 456
C 452
C 448
C 442
Av 1
Av 2
Av 3
Av 4
Av 5

Av de las
Américas

Via Blanca

Playa
Boca
Ciega

Av de las Terrazas

Laguna
Itabo

Av 4
Av 6

Straits of Florida

Via Blanca

C 22
Av1
C 19
C 14
C 13
C 12
C 11
C 10
C 9

Av de las
Banderas

Overview

Straits of Florida

Rio Guanabo
Campo
Florido

Main Map

Playa El Mégano Straits of Florida
Playa Tarará
Guanabo

Bacuranao
Via Blanca

ALAMAR
Cojimar
Via Monumental

Embalse
Bacuranao

Havana

10 km
5 miles

Alamar

Rio Cojímar

Doble Vía

Cojimar

Torreón de
Cojímar
C 96
C C
C-1-B
C-3
Av Central
Los pinos
C 152
Martí

COJIMAR

Sights

Havana Kiteboarding Club
KITESURFING

1 Map p102, A1

At Tarará, where conditions for kiteboarding are excellent, this Italian-run operator offers lessons (CUC$155 for two hours) and board rental (CUC$60 per hour), and can organize accommodation packages in the adjacent Villa Tarará. (58-04-96-56; www.havanakite.com; Plaza Cobre, btwn 12 & 14, Tarará)

Marlin Náutica Tarará
WATER SPORTS

2 Map p102, A1

Yacht charters, deep-sea fishing and scuba diving are offered at the Marina Tarará, 22km east of Havana. It's generally easier to organize activities at a hotel tour desk in Havana before heading out. Prices are similar to those at Marina Hemingway. (7-796-0240; cnr Av 8 & Calle 17, Tarará)

Torreón de Cojímar
FORT

3 Map p102, A3

Overlooking the harbor is an old Spanish fort (1649) presently occupied by the Cuban Coast Guard. It was the first fortification taken by the British when they attacked Havana from the rear in 1762. Next to this tower and framed by a neoclassical archway is a gilded bust of Ernest Hemingway, erected by the residents of Cojímar in 1962.

Local Life
Cojímar

Situated 10km east of Havana is the little port town of Cojímar, famous for harboring Ernest Hemingway's fishing boat *El Pilar* in the 1940s and 1950s. These days it's an obligatory stop on any 'Hemingway-was-here' tour, with groups arriving primarily to visit the historic if mediocre Restaurante la Terraza where Ernesto once sank daiquiris.

Alamar
AREA

4 Map p102, B3

East across the river from Cojímar is a large housing estate of prefabricated apartment blocks built from 1971 by *micro brigadas* (small armies of workers who built post-revolution housing). This is the birthplace of Cuban rap, and the annual hip-hop festival is still centered here. It is also the home of one of Cuba's largest and most successful urban agricultural gardens, the **Organopónico Vivero Alamar**.

Eating

Il Piccolo
ITALIAN $$

5 Map p102, E2

This Guanabo old-school private restaurant has been around for eons and is a bit of an open secret among *habaneros,* some of whom consider its thin-crust wood-oven pizzas to be the best in Cuba. Out of the way and a little more expensive than Playas del Este's other numerous pizza joints, it's well worth the journey – take a horse and cart on Av 5. (📞7-796-4300; cnr Av 5 & Calle 502; pizzas CUC$7-9; 🕙noon-11pm)

Chicken Little   INTERNATIONAL $$

6 🍴 Map p102, E2

Forgive them the kitschy name – Chicken Little could yet make it big. Defying Guanabo's ramshackle image, this deluxe restaurant has polite wait-staff with welcome cocktails who'll talk you through a menu of pesto chicken, chicken in orange and honey and – surprise – some jolly fine lobster. (📞7-796-2351; Calle 504 No 5815, btwn Calles 5b & 5c; mains CUC$6-9; 🕙noon-11pm)

Don Pepe   SEAFOOD $

7 🍴 Map p102, A1

When the Guanabo pizza gets too much, head to this thatched-roof, beach-style restaurant about 50m from the sand. It specializes in sea-food. (Av de las Terrazas; mains CUC$5-7; 🕙10am-11pm)

Restaurante
421   INTERNATIONAL, CUBAN $$

8 🍴 Map p102, D2

Ask a local about food preferences in Guanabo and they'll probably direct you up the steep hill behind the main roundabout to this newish perch that has a surprisingly wide selection of

DPA PICTURE ALLIANCE/ALAMY ©

Restaurante la Terraza (p105)

Cuban favorites mixed with international dishes, including paella and the inevitable pizza. Sit indoors or outside and enjoy attentive service amid a perfect fusion of food and people. (☎53-05-69-00; Calle 462 No 911, btwn Avs 9 & 11; mains CUC$5-12; ⏱9am-1am)

Restaurante la Terraza SEAFOOD $$

| 9 | 🍴 | Map p102, A4 |

Another photo-adorned shrine to the ghost of Hemingway, Restaurante la Terraza specializes in seafood and does a roaring trade from the hordes of Papa fans who get bused in daily. The food is surprisingly mediocre, although the terrace dining room overlooking the bay is pleasant. More atmospheric is the old bar out front, where mojitos haven't yet reached El Floridita rates. (Calle 152 No 161, Cojímar; meals CUC$7-15; ⏱noon-11pm)

Drinking

Bar Luna BAR

| 10 | 🍸 | Map p102, D2 |

New and privately run, Bar Luna is also a restaurant, but with its luminously lit interior and open terrace overlooking the street it's probably best utilized for its drinks and nighttime action. This being Guanabo, you can expect to see plenty of foreign men of a

✅ **Top Tip**
Local Transport

Forget cars in Guanabo. Most of the locals cover short distances in the ubiquitous horses and carts that act as the neighborhood's taxis. Follow their example and flag one down on Av 5. For die-hards, a unique way of getting to Guanabo is by the electric Hershey train that departs from Casablanca station on the eastern side of Havana harbor. From Guanabo station, it's a 3km walk to the beach.

certain age and their Cuban escorts. (Av 5, btwn Calles 482 & 484; ⏱8am-3am)

Entertainment

Centro Cultural Enguayabera ARTS CENTER

| 11 | ⭐ | Map p102, B4 |

In an old shirt factory, abandoned in the 1990s when it became a rubbish dump and public urinal, is this new state-sponsored community arts project in lowly Alamar, inspired by the Fábrica de Arte Cubano (p83) in Vedado. It bivouacs numerous funky venues under its cultural umbrella, including three small cinemas, a literary cafe, a theater and a crafts outlet. (Calle 162, btwn Avs 7a & 7b, Alamar; ⏱9am-11pm)

Explore

Regla & Guanabacoa

Regla and Guanabacoa are two small towns on the eastern side of Havana harbor that got swallowed up during Havana's urban growth. Slow-paced and little visited by tourists, the municipalities retain an independent-minded and culturally distinct spirit. Guanabacoa is some-times called *el pueblo embrujado* ('the bewitched town') for its strong Santería traditions. Regla has equally potent religious affiliations.

The Sights in a Day

☀ Have a good breakfast in Habana Vieja before taking the short 10-minute ferry ride across the harbor. Sitting directly opposite the dock in Regla and intrinsically tied to the sea is **Iglesia de Nuestra Señora de Regla** (p108), the neighborhood's most symbolic sight – a place of pilgrimage for Catholics and adherents of Santería alike. You can follow the religious theme around the corner to the **Museo Municipal de Regla** (p114), with exhibits focusing on Santería deities.

☀ It's possible to cover the 3km between Regla and Guanabacoa on foot or by (P-15) bus. Walkers can divert to the **Colina Lenin** (p114) for impressive harbor views on the way. Of Guanabacoa's meager lunch offerings, **La Brisilla** (p115) wins by a mile. Afterwards, head to pivotal Parque Martí where you can try raising the pastor to let you in the **Iglesia de Guanabacoa** (p114) or shrug off the officious 'guides' in the **Museo Municipal de Guanabacoa** (p114).

☾ Evenings in Guanabacoa are generally low-key, but you might get lucky with some athletic rumba dancing in the **Centro Cultural Recreativo los Orishas** (p117).

For a local's day in Guanabacoa, see p110.

 Top Sights

Iglesia de Nuestra Señora de Regla (p108)

◯ **Local Life**

Guanabacoa (p110)

♥ **Best of Havana**

Historic Sites
Ermita de Potosí (p111)

Iglesia de Nuestra Señora de Regla (p108)

Getting There & Away

🚌 **Bus** Metro bus P-15 from the Parque de la Fraternidad in Centro Habana goes to Regla and Guanabacoa, stopping at the main train terminal in Habana Vieja on the way.

⚓ **Ferry** Regla is easily accessible on the passenger ferry that departs every 20 minutes (CUC$0.25) from the Emboque de Luz at the intersection of San Pedro and Santa Clara in Habana Vieja.

Top Sights
Iglesia de Nuestra Señora de Regla

As important as it is diminutive, this modest church on the eastern shores of Havana harbor shelters the blessed virgin of Regla worshipped by Catholics and adherents of Santeria (who call her Yemaya) with equal fervor. The virgin's statue was brought to Havana in the 1690s and harks back to a devotional cult that originated in Spain in the 5th century.

👁 Map p112, A2

🕑 7:30am-6pm

The Church

The settlement of Regla grew up around a shrine first built here in 1687. The church went through various incarnations until the current structure was erected in 1810, by which time the virgin had been declared the patron saint of the port of Havana. The chapel-like building with its blue wooden doors, and heavy ceiling beams is colonial in style. Inside, alcoves reveal statues of the saints and a gold-leaf altar is dominated by a depiction of the black virgin in her customary blue robes.

Venerated Virgin

The virgin, represented by a black Madonna, is venerated in the Catholic faith and associated in the Santería religion with Yemayá, the orisha of the ocean and the patron of sailors (always represented in blue). Legend claims that this image was carved by St Augustine 'The African' in the 5th century, and that in AD 453 a disciple brought the statue to Spain to safeguard it from barbarians. The small vessel in which the image was traveling survived a storm in the Strait of Gibraltar, so the figure was recognized as the patron of sailors. In more recent times, Cuban rafters attempting to reach the US have also evoked the protection of the Black Virgin.

Vendors

It is rare to find the church empty. Pilgrims regularly file in to pray quietly and offer gifts to the virgin. A semipermanent posse of vendors awaits outside the church selling flowers, trinkets and Santería dolls. Some of them lay out tarot cards and offer to tell fortunes

☑ **Top Tips**

▶ For full Regla immersion, visit on September 7th, the virgin's feast day, when the statue is taken from the church and paraded around the neighborhood.

▶ To broaden your knowledge of Santería stroll up to the Museo Municipal de Regla (p114) after visiting the church.

✗ **Take a Break**

▶ There is very little in the way of good restaurants in Regla.

▶ The new **Emboque de Luz** (Map p34, D6) ferry dock (on the Habana Vieja side of the harbor) has a reasonable cafe selling drinks and light snacks.

Local Life
Guanabacoa

Few travelers take the time to penetrate Guanabacoa, a dense urban neighborhood whose fabled past is overlaid by a gritty contemporary exterior. Once an indigenous town, later a hotbed of resistance, still a stronghold of the Santeria religion; it's a neighborhood with a layered history crying out for a face-lift. But, with a little imagination, anyone can delve in and explore.

❶ **Parque de la República**
Entering Guanabacoa from the west, it's easy to overlook **Parque de la República**, a former military parade ground that, these days, is dominated by a sunken Greco-Roman style amphitheater built after the revolution in 1960. The alfresco structure hosts sporadic local happenings including music performances, dance and live theater.

2 Parque Martí

The hub of the neighborhood is the slightly scruffy but unashamedly perky **Parque Martí**, overlooked by the local church which, on the rare occasions it opens its doors, reveals precious baroque art. Linger on a bench and you'll quickly find yourself absorbing a slice of street life seemingly a million miles from tourist-crammed central Havana.

3 Calle Pepe Antonio

No exploration of Guanabacoa should conclude without a call-out to local hero, Pepe Antonio, the battling mayor who led the resistance against the invading British army in 1762. In **Calle Pepe Antonio**, the street named in his honor, local life battles on amid the disheveled buildings. At No 13 is the currently closed Cine-Teatro Carral, with interesting Arabic embellishments.

4 Convento de Santo Domingo

Locals regularly lament the state of the sadly blemished **Convento de Santo Domingo** (Santo Domingo No 407, Guanabacoa), which urgently needs money and attention to prevent its collapse. The muscular baroque building has survived plenty of knocks in its 280-year history, including occupation by the British in the 1760s. Inside, the ornate altarpiece is dedicated to the locally venerated Virgin of Candelaría.

5 Liceo

Guanabacoa has contributed grandly to Havana's cultural life throughout its long history and its former Liceo (a club for writers and artists) – today the **Casa de Cultura Rita Montaner** (Máximo Gómez, cnr Nazareno) – remains a place where you might catch an exposition, live performance or passing troubadour. Founded in 1861, this was where José Martí made his first public speech in Cuba.

6 Ermita de Potosí

The diminutive **Ermita de Potosí** (cnr Calzada Vieja Guanabacoa & Potosí; ⊙8am-5pm) doesn't really advertise itself as the oldest ecclesial building in Cuba, but, dating from 1675, that's exactly what it is. It's also one of the few historical structures in Guanabacoa that has been meaningfully renovated.

0 500 m
0 0.25 miles

Bahía
de la
Habana

**Iglesia de
Nuestra Señora
de Regla**

Martí

Galería
César Leal

La Piedra 1

Ambrón

**Museo
Municipal
de Regla** 4

27 de Noviembre

Parque
Guaicanamar

Martí

Albuquerque

Presno

Lenín

REGLA

Martí

24 de Febrero

Colina
Lenín 5

Independencia

Calzada de Regla

Vía Blanca

Primer Anillo del Puerto

Casablanca
(5.5km)

For reviews see
- ⊙ Top Sights — p108
- ⊚ Sights — p114
- ✕ Eating — p115
- 🍷 Drinking — p117

Guanabacoa
Train
Station

Rosalina

Vía Blanca

Cruz Verde

Santo Domingo

Venus

Fernando Fuero (Amargura)

Iglesia de
Guanabacoa

Quintín Banderas

E V Valenzuela

Parque
Martí

Rafael de Cárdenas

Adolfo Del Castillo Cadenas

Lamas

Segui

Máximo Gómez

Maceo

Santa Ana

Pepe Antonio

GUANABACOA

Museo de
Mártires

Martí

E Guiral

Bertematti

Nazareno

Aranguren

Independencia

Museo
Municipal de
Guanabacoa

Independencia

Calzada de Guanabacoa

Miguel Coyula

Sights

Galería César Leal
GALLERY

1 Map p112, A3

Humble Regla has a small gallery and an art school overseen by noted Cuban artist César Leal (b 1948). It holds regular expositions by the students or – if you're lucky – the artist himself. Alternatively, you can see Leal's work in the Museo Nacional de Bellas Artes. (Martí 221, btwn Ambrón & La Piedra; admission free; ⏱hours vary)

Museo Municipal de Guanabacoa
MUSEUM

2 Map p112, G3

Guanabacoa's main museum, like Regla's, is an important shrine to Santería, though you'll need to see past the rundown facilities and impassive 'guides' to appreciate it. The collection is small but concise; rooms are dedicated to the various Santería deities with a particular focus on the *orisha* Elegguá. Equally fascinating are rare artifacts from the Palo Monte and Abakuá religions. (Martí No 108; CUC$2; ⏱9am-5:30pm Tue-Sat, 9am-1pm Sun)

Iglesia de Guanabacoa
CHURCH

3 Map p112, G3

This church, in Parque Martí in the center of Guanabacoa, is also known as the Iglesia de Nuestra Señora de la Asunción, and was designed by Lorenzo Camacho and built between 1721 and 1748 with a Moorish-influenced wooden ceiling. (cnr Pepe Antonio & Adolfo del Castillo Cadenas; ⏱parochial office 8-11am & 2-5pm Mon-Fri)

Museo Municipal de Regla
MUSEUM

4 Map p112, A3

If you've come across to see Regla's church, you should also check out this important museum. Don't be put off by its superficial dinginess – there's some valuable relics inside. Located a few blocks up the main street from the ferry, it records Regla's history and Afro-Cuban religions. Don't miss the Palo Monte *ngangas* (cauldrons) and the masked Abakuá dancing figurines. (Martí No 158; CUC$2; ⏱9am-5pm Mon-Sat, 9am-noon Sun)

Colina Lenin
MONUMENT

5 Map p112, C4

From Regla's boat dock, head straight (south) on Martí past Parque Guaicanamar, and turn left on Albuquerque and right on 24 de Febrero, the road to Guanabacoa. About 1.5km

---

☑ Top Tip

Ferry Ride
The ferry to Regla is a classic non-tourist Havana experience. There isn't even a tourist fare; you pay in *moneda nacional*, or, failing that, the smallest CUC$ coin in your possession.

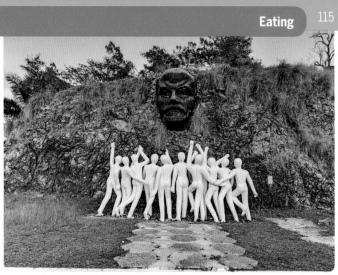

Colina Lenin (p114)

from the ferry you'll see a high metal stairway that gives access to Colina Lenin, one of two Havana monuments to Vladimir Ilyich Ulyanov (better known to his friends and enemies as Lenin).

Museo de Mártires
MUSEUM

6 ⊙ Map p112, F4

Effectively an arm of Guanabacoa's municipal museum, this place is on the road to Regla and displays a scruffy selection of material relevant to the revolution and the locals who fought in it. In a glass case there's a suit once worn by José Martí, who made his first public speech in Gua-

nabacoa in 1879. (Martí No 320; admission free; ⊙10am-6pm Tue-Sat, 9am-1pm Sun)

Eating

La Brisilla
CUBAN $$

7 ✖ Map p112, F3

Unsignposted, hard to find and, consequently, almost 100% local, this is a rare private restaurant in Guanabacoa, where the food culture doesn't seem to have moved on much since the not-so-tasty '90s. You'll have to ask the way in Spanish to get here, but when and if you make it, the rabbit in red wine and succulent lobster will leave you feeling as pleased as you'll

Understand

Santería

- -

You'll appreciate and enjoy Regla and Guanabacoa more if you learn a little about the sometimes complex mysteries of Santería before you arrive.

A syncretistic religion that hides African roots beneath a symbolic Catholic veneer, Santería is a product of the slave era, but remains deeply embedded in contemporary Cuban culture where it has had a major impact on the evolution of the country's music, dance and rituals. Today, over three million Cubans identify as believers, including numerous writers, artists and politicians.

Santería's misrepresentations start with its name; the word is a historical misnomer first coined by Spanish colonizers to describe the 'saint worship' practiced by 19th-century African slaves. A more accurate moniker is Regla de Ocha (way of the *orishas*), or Lucumí, named for the original adherents who hailed from the Yoruba ethno-linguistic group in southwestern Nigeria, a prime looting ground for slave-traders.

Fully initiated adherents of Santería (called *santeros*) believe in one God known as Oludomare, the creator of the universe and the source of Ashe (all life forces on earth). Rather than interact with the world directly, Oludomare communicates through a pantheon of *orishas*, various imperfect deities similar to Catholic saints or Greek gods, who are blessed with different natural (water, weather, metals) and human (love, intellect, virility) qualities. *Orishas* have their own feast days, demand their own food offerings, and are given numbers and colors to represent their personalities.

Santería's syncretism with Catholicism occurred surreptitiously during the colonial era when African animist traditions were banned. In order to hide their faith from the Spanish authorities, African slaves secretly twinned their *orishas* with Catholic saints. Thus, Changó the male *orisha* of thunder and lightning was hidden behind the form of Santa Bárbara, while Elegguá, the *orisha* of travel and roads became St Anthony de Padua. In this way an erstwhile slave praying before a statue of Santa Bárbara was clandestinely offering their respects to Changó, while Afro-Cubans ostensibly celebrating the feast day of Our Lady of Regla (September 7) were, in reality, honoring Yemayá. This syncretization, though no longer strictly necessary, is still followed today.

be surprised. (Cruz Verde, btwn Santa Ana & Segui; mains CUC$6-10; ⏲noon-midnight)

Dulcinea

BAKERY $

8 Map p112, G3

By the time you get to Guanabacoa, you'll likely be starving (especially if you've walked over from the Regla neighborhood), so the simple cakes in this home-town Cuban bakery will probably look appetizing. Make the most of them; there's not much else in these parts. (Adolfo del Castillo Cadenas No 5, cnr Pepe Antonio; snacks CUC$1-2; ⏲8am-6pm)

Drinking

Centro Cultural Recreativo los Orishas

BAR

9 Map p112, G4

Situated in the hotbed of Havana's Santería community in Guanabacoa, this bar-restaurant used to host live rumba music on weekends, including regular visits from the Conjunto Folklórico Nacional, though it seemed to have limited its program at last visit. The walled garden bar is surrounded by Afro-Cuban sculptures of various Santería deities. (☎7-794-7878; Martí No 175, btwn Lamas & Cruz Verde; ⏲10am-2am)

Local Life

Regla Streetlife

A largely working-class neighborhood notable for its large thermoelectric power plant and shipyard, Regla is almost free of tourist trappings. Walk up Calle Martí and drink in Havana from a totally different perspective: a confusing melee of asthmatic Ladas, weather-beaten shops, and a food culture that seems to be stuck in 1995.

Top Sights
Museo Hemingway

Getting There

🚌 **Metro Bus** The P-7 from Parque de la Fraternidad in Centro Habana stops on the main road just outside the museum. Bus P-2 uses the same stop and runs to and from Vedado.

Cuba wasn't a passing dalliance for American writer, Ernest Hemingway. The well-traveled novelist lived in the Finca la Vigía in the tranquil Havana suburb of San Francisco de Paula for more than two decades starting in 1939. When he departed, tired and depressed, for the US in 1960, soon after the Castro revolution, he generously donated his house to the 'Cuban people.'

La Torre (p119)

Don't Miss

La Casona

The main attraction at the so-called Museo Hemingway is the house itself, an attractive single-story abode full of natural light and open, spacious rooms. To prevent the pilfering of objects, visitors are not allowed inside the house, but there are enough open doors and windows to allow a proper glimpse into Papa's unusual universe. Not surprisingly, there are books everywhere (including beside the toilet), a large Victrola and record collection, and an alarming number of animal heads.

La Torre

The three-story tower next to Hemingway's main house was where the author came to relax, ruminate and sometimes write. It contains a tiny typewriter, a telescope, a comfortable lounger and plenty of dusty books. The view north toward the distant city is suitably inspiring.

The Pool & Pérgola

You'll need to use a little imagination to refill Hemingway's elegant swimming pool with water and summon up the ghost of actress Ava Gardner swimming naked in it. Alternatively, you can just collapse onto a chaise lounge and enjoy the whispering palms and craning bamboo that grows so fast you can practically hear it. Two bathhouses either side of the traditional *pérgola* contain interesting photos of Hemingway and his guests enjoying booze and book talk by the pool.

Pilar

The *Pilar* was Hemingway's beloved wooden fishing boat that he once kept moored at the nearby fishing village of Cojímar. Today, it sits in dry dock next to the swimming pool.

☎ 7-692-0176

cnr Vígia & Singer

CUC$5

🕙 10am-4:30pm
Mon-Sat

☑ Top Tips

▶ Don't come if it's raining as most of the sights are outdoors and sometimes closed in inclement weather.

▶ For full Hemingway immersion you can partake in a Hemingway tour. Havana Super Tour (p61) offers a good option that takes in the museum along with many of the writer's favorite Havana drinking holes.

✗ Take a Break

The Museum complex has its own small alfresco cafeteria selling mainly drinks. Make the most of it; there's little else to whet the appetite in these parts.

The Best of
Havana

Havana's Best Walks

Havana's Best...

Callejón de Hamel (p55)
ALISON ECKETT/ALAMY ©

Best Walks
Architecture on the Prado

🏃 The Walk

This walk takes in the whole of Paseo del Prado along with many of the sumptuous buildings that overlook it. With a tree-lined walkway running down its center, Prado has an intentionally European flavor. Conceived in the late 1700s, it has since developed into one of the city's most handsome thoroughfares.

Start: Malecón & Prado

Finish: Capitolio Nacional

Length: 1.6km; 45 minutes

🍴 Take a Break

Parque Central, three-quarters of the way into this walk, is ringed by some of Havana's finest hotels. While they might be out of the price range of many visitors, they're still good places to sink a drink in plush often historic surroundings. **Hotel Iberostar Parque Central** and **Hotel Saratoga** are both good options.

Edificio Bacardí (p36)

❶ Teatro Fausto

From the northern end of the Prado, head south toward Parque Central, passing the streamlined art deco **Teatro Fausto**. Dating from 1938, it exhibits the sharp lines and pure cubist simplicity of Depression-era America.

❷ Hotel Sevilla

Contrasting sharply with other modern architectural styles on Calle Trocadero is the neo-Moorish **Hotel Sevilla**, built in 1908, but harking back to a bygone age of Spanish stucco and intricate *mudéjar* craftsmanship.

❸ Edifico Bacardí

Turn right on Agramonte and detour down Ánimas for Havana's most emblematic art deco building, **Edificio Bacardí** (p36), the ex-headquarters of the Bacardi rum dynasty. It's a vivid incarnation of this popular interwar architectural genre.

❹ Palacio de los Matrimonios

Retrace Ánimas to the Prado and you'll be

eyeballing the **Palacio de los Matrimonios**, a rival to the presidential palace for opulence. Dating from the 1910s, it was once the Casino Español, a Cuban-Spanish social club. These days it hosts weddings in its lavish 1st-floor ballroom.

5 Gran Teatro de la Habana Alicia Alonso

At the southwest corner of Parque Central, eclecticism meets neo-baroque at the flamboyant Centro Gallego, another Spanish social club, built in 1915 around the existing Teatro Tacón. Today, after a lengthy restoration, it's the **Gran Teatro de la Habana Alicia Alonso** (p63).

6 Museo Nacional de Bellas Artes

Facing the theater across leafy Parque Central is the equally eclectic Centro Asturiano, now part of the **Museo Nacional de Bellas Artes** (p50), with four separate rooftop lookouts and a richly gilded interior.

7 Capitolio Nacional

Restoration is ongoing at the Cuban national assembly, **Capitolio Nacional** (p58), built between 1926 and 1929 on sugar money.

It captures Latin America's neoclassical revival, with sweeping stairways and Doric columns harking back to a purer and more strident Grecian ideal.

Best Walks
The Malecón

🏃 The Walk

Havana's 7km-long Malecón is one of the world's great sea drives and, without doubt, the city's most quintessential walk. Sometimes dubbed 'the world's longest sofa', this is where the whole city comes to meet, greet, date and debate.

Start: Malecón & Prado

Finish: Malecón & Paseo

Length: 5.5km; two hours

🍴 Take a Break

Once a culinary desert, the Malecón has recently sprouted some decent bars and restaurants. Perhaps the most heralded to date is the Russian-themed **Nazdarovie** (p61) on the upper floor of an ocean-facing tenement not far from the junction with El Prado.

Antonio Maceo Statue

❶ Castillo de San Salvador de la Punta

Marking the beginning of the Malecón, the 16th-century fort of **Castillo de San Salvador de la Punta** (p38) predates the sea drive by three centuries. It guards the entrance to Havana harbor and its thick limestone walls face off against the larger Morro fort opposite. The broad esplanade abutting the ocean is a favorite spot for lovers and fishers.

❷ Antonio Maceo Statue

The first break in the sea drive heading west is a small park with a dashing **statue** of Antonio Maceo, the Cuban Independence war hero, atop his horse. Behind the park rises the concrete mass of the Hospital Nacional Hermanos Ameijeiras. An underpass links the park to the walkway.

❸ Hotel Nacional

Raised on a rocky knoll known as the Loma de Taganana, the **Hotel Nacional** (p74) dominates the Malecón at the intersection with La Rampa. Far more than just a hotel, it's also a national monument, a top cabaret venue, and possibly the best place in Cuba to sit on a breeze-caressed terrace and enjoy rum and cigars.

4 Monumento a las Víctimas del Maine

A rare monument honoring Americans in Cuba, **Monumento a las Víctimas del Maine** (p76) commemorates the 266 US Marines killed when the US battleship *Maine* exploded in Havana harbor in 1898, an incident that helped spark the Spanish-American War. An eagle atop the monument was toppled in 1959 during a moment of high revolutionary fervor.

5 US Embassy

The former US Interests Section office was converted back into the **US Embassy** in 2015, and the Stars and Stripes fly here once again. The political propaganda boards that used to dominate the immediate environs have quietly disappeared, although the parade ground in front is still called the Tribuna Anti-Imperialista José Martí.

6 Hotel Riviera

Still further west along the Malecón, end your walk at the striking modernist **Hotel Riviera** that was opened in 1957 as the property of US gangster Meyer Lansky. Recently taken over by Iberostar, the hotel retains the over-the-top design of its brief 1950s heyday.

Best
Live Music

Welcome to one of the most musically diverse cities on the planet, where guitars still outnumber MP3 players and singing is seen as just another form of verbal communication. The traditional genres of son and salsa are merely one groove on a larger record. Cuba has been pushing the musical envelope for decades. From Benny Moré to hip hop, the city bleeds syncopated rhythms.

Into the Mix

Aside from the obvious Spanish and African roots, Cuban music has drawn upon a number of other influences. Mixed into an already exotic melting pot are genres from France, the US, Haiti and Jamaica. Conversely, Cuban music has also played a key role in developing various melodic styles and movements in other parts of the world. In Spain they called this process *ida y vuelta* (return trip) and it is most clearly evident in a style of flamenco called *guajira*. Elsewhere the 'Cuban effect' can be traced back to forms as diverse as New Orleans jazz, New York salsa and West African Afrobeat.

Rumba

Raw, expressive and exciting to watch, Cuban rumba is a spontaneous and often informal affair performed by groups of up to a dozen musicians. Conga drums, claves, *palitos* (sticks), *marugas* (iron shakers) and *cajones* (packing cases) lay out the interlocking rhythms, while the vocals alternate between a wildly improvising lead singer and an answering *coro* (chorus).

LUCAS VALLECILLOS/ALAMY ©

☑ Top Tips

▶ A lack of decent rock-music venues in the 1990s meant that denizens of Havana's roquero (rock music) subculture were forced to hang around on street corners – more specifically the corner of Calles 23 and G in Vedado – to discuss AC/DC guitar riffs and Led Zeppelin song meanings. Plenty still linger.

Live Music Venues

Fábrica de Arte Cubano
A potluck of performance art from male choirs to female jazz jams. (p83)

Jazz Café The best live jazz in the capital. (p83)

Salón Rosado Benny Moré (p91)

Café Teatro Bertolt Brecht Where Havana's 'yoof' queue up on Wednesday nights to see live bands such as Interactivo. (p71)

Casa de la Música Of Havana's two music 'casas' this one in Miramar is probably the most sophisticated. (p97)

Salón Rosado Benny Moré Young, cool, very local Playa neighborhood club with compulsory dancing. (p91)

Bars with Live Music

El Patchanka Fusion rock raises the rafters at this agreeably dog-eared dive bar in Plaza del Cristo. (p44)

Café Cantante Mi Habana Multifarious club and music venue in Cuba's National Theater complex. (p71)

Espacios Old Fashioned Bohemian abode where musicians casually stroll in and let rip around 10:30-ish. (p45)

Rumba

Callejón de Hamel The soul of Afro-Cuban society takes to the street on Sundays for rumba drumming. (p55; pictured left)

Centro Cultural El Gran Palenque Athletic folkloric dance shows, including rumba, showcased by one of Cuba's finest dance troupes. (p83)

Jazz

Jazz Café Havana's suavest jazz venue offers a dinner show with ocean views. (p83)

Jazz Club la Zorra y el Cuervo Hot, intense underground club where free jazz is king. (p83)

Café Miramar Havana's newest jazz club is building a lofty reputation out in the Playa neighborhood (p96)

Traditional Cuban

El Hurón Azul Boleros, son and trova peacefully coexist at the HQ of the Cuban writers and artist's union. (p71)

El Gato Tuerto Where baby-boomers come to relive their youth. (p84)

El Guajirito Old-school singers belting out Benny Moré era *boleros*. (p65)

Best
Nightlife & Entertainment

Although it may have lost its pre-revolutionary reputation as a dazzling casino quarter, Vedado is still the place for nightlife in Havana. Cabaret, jazz, classical music, dance and cinema are offered in abundance and it's invariably of a high standard. Entertainment in Habana Vieja is emerging from a Rip Van Winkle–like slumber and becoming increasingly hip. Centro's nightlife is edgier and more local.

BONNIE CATON/ALAMY ©

Cuban Dance Fusion

Cuban dance is as hybridized as the country's music; indeed, many dance genres evolved from popular strands of Cuban music.

Early dance forms mimicked the European-style ballroom dances practiced by the colonizers, but added African elements. This unorthodox amalgamation of styles can be seen in esoteric genres such as the French-Haitian tumba francesa, a marriage between 18th-century French court dances and imported African rhythms: dancers wearing elegant dresses wave fans and handkerchiefs while shimmying to the drum patterns of Nigeria and Benin. Other dances reflected the working lives of Cuban slaves.

The first truly popular dance hybrid was the danzón, a sequence dance involving couples whose origins lay in the French and English *contradanza*, but whose rhythm contained a distinctive African syncopation.

The mambo and *chachachá* evolved the danzón further, creating dances that were more improvised and complicated. Mambo's creator, Pérez Prado, specifically pioneered mambo dancing to fit his new music in the 1940s while the *chachachá* was codified as a ballroom dance in the early 1950s by a Frenchman named Monsieur Pierre.

Entertaining Nights Out

Fábrica de Arte Cubano
A 'factory of creativity' might sound like a contradiction in terms until you check this place out. (p83)

Gran Teatro de la Habana Alicia Alonso
Havana headquarters for ballet, opera and musicals. (p63)

Jazz Café Havana's suavest jazz venue offers a dinner show with ocean views. (p83)

Tropicana Nightclub
Havana's oldest and most iconic cabaret show has been going for around 80 years. (p96; pictured above)

Cabaret

Tropicana Nightclub
It's expensive and there

Fábrica de Arte Cubano (p83)

are lots of tourists, but that doesn't stop it being good. (p96)

Cabaret Parisién A thoroughly decent alternative to the Tropicana that kicks off nightly in the Hotel Nacional. (p83)

Habana Café Tourist-heavy cabaret in the Hotel Meliá Cohiba in a retro American setting. (p85)

Nightclubs

Casa de la Música Live music and dexterous dancing by highly-coordinated locals. (p65)

Piano Bar Delirio Habanero Hugely varied repertoires characterize this suave club overlooking Plaza de la Revolución. (p81)

Cabaret Las Vegas Havana's best drag shows. (p81)

Salsa Dancing

El Salón Chévere Pulsing salsa dance-club in the forest beside the Almendares River. (p96)

Bar-Restaurante 1830 Refined restaurant where clients kick their shoes off after dinner. (p80)

El Guajirito Legendary Buena Vista Social Club singers encourage spontaneous dancing. (p65)

Cinemas & Theaters

Teatro América Hosts a variety of comedy, dance, jazz and salsa shows. (p65)

Teatro Nacional de Cuba Hosts landmark concerts, foreign theater troupes and La Colmenita children's company. (p85)

Casa de las Americas Offers conferences, exhibitions, a gallery, a bookstore and concerts, as well as its own annual literary award (p84)

Centro Cultural Enguayabera A new state-sponsored community arts project that includes three small cinemas, a literary cafe, a theater and a crafts outlet. (p105)

Cine Yara The first date of many an enamored *cubano* has taken place at this classic modernist cinema on Vedado's main crossroads. (p71)

Best
Drinking

Havana's contingent of bars has exploded in recent years with the city adding plenty of new private places plying Cuba's default cocktails (mojitos and daiquiris) and its strongly brewed home-grown coffee. Some double up as art galleries, others turn into live music venues as the night wears on, but all are heavy with that unique, gloriously hedonistic Havana atmosphere.

Cool Cafes & Bohemian Bars

Havana is going through an interesting stage at present. Private enterprise is showing the first flowerings of a creative spring, while the big-name brands from that well-known 'frenemy' in the north have yet to gain a foothold. As a result, the city is rife with experimentation. Here a dandy cafe decked out like a bohemian artist's lair, there a trancey lounge bar where earnest travelers sit around comparing Che Guevara T-shirts. Maybe it's something they put in the mojitos, but the face of Cuban cafe culture has never looked so good.

Rum Masters

Rum is made from molasses, a by-product of sugarcane. Its fabrication in Cuba has been overseen by generations of skillful *maestros romeros* (rum masters) who must have a minimum of 15 years of rum-tasting experience. The drink is classified by both color (dark, golden or clear) and age *(añejo)*. Good rums can range from three to 14 years in age. As a rule, rum cocktails (always made with clear rum) are more popular with tourists than Cubans, who prefer to drink their rum dark and neat (without ice) in order to enjoy the full flavor.

GEORGIA WESTLAKE/ALAMY ©

☑ Top Tips

▶ The 'holy trinity' of Cuban cocktails consists of the mojito (rum, sugar, lime, soda and mint), the daiquiri (shaved ice, rum, citrus juice and sweetener) and the Cuba Libre (rum, lime and cola).

▶ *Guarapo* is pure sugarcane juice mixed with ice and lemon and served from quaint little roadside stalls called *guaraperos* all over Cuba.

Atmospheric bars

Café Madrigal Trendy abode with distracting art and romantic lighting in a leafy part of Vedado. (p80)

La Bodeguita del Medio (p45)

Azúcar Lounge Poised like a theater box suspended above Plaza Vieja and offering great coffee and cocktails. (p42)

El Chanchullero Appetite-quenching tapas, cheap cocktails and cool people. (p44)

El Dandy If ever a cafe suited its name, this is it. (p42)

Coffee bars

Café Arcangel Small, original, one-of-a-kind cafe in a tatty Centro Habana street. (p62)

Café Fortuna Joe Weirdest cafe in Havana – no contest. You can even imbibe your *cafecito* while sitting on a toilet seat! (p91)

Cafe Presidente Brings a fine cup of the caffeinated stuff to accompany your breakfast. (p77)

El Dandy Strong coffee, interesting people, head-turning wall art and top-notch service. (p42)

'Hemingway was here' bars

La Bodeguita del Medio Brave the chaos just once at the cradle of the mojito (and shrine to Ernest Hemingway). (p45)

El Floridita Get your photo taken next to a statue of Hemingway and sink an obligatory daiquiri. (p44; pictured left)

Sloppy Joe's Don't worry! It's not at all sloppy and the owner is no longer called Joe. (p62)

Bar Dos Hermanos Follow in the footsteps of a long queue of writers and artists (the plaque on the wall tells all). (p45)

Cocktails

Chill Out Lounge on a sofa on the roof of this refined Vedado mansion. (p81)

Café Madrigal Cocktail art in a pretty and undeniably pretentious setting. (p80)

Café Mamainé Where the locals artists go for their cheap mojitos. (p80)

Best
Food

Havana's eating scene has progressed exponentially in recent years, thanks to new laws governing private enterprise. The most condensed scene is in Habana Vieja. Playa, thanks to its diplomatic heritage, has traditionally harbored the city's most exclusive restaurants. Culinary experimentation has also proliferated. You can now find specialist Russian, Korean, Chinese, Iranian and Italian restaurants.

YAACOV DAGAN/ALAMY ©

Stewing 500 Years

Cuba's cuisine is a creative stew of selective morsels, recipes and cooking techniques left behind by successive travelers since the epoch of Columbus and Velázquez. Imagine a bubbling cauldron that has been filled with ingredients plucked from Spain, Africa, France, pre-colonial Taínos, and cultures from various other islands in the Caribbean, and left to intermingle and marinate for 500 years.

From the original Taínos came indigenous root vegetables such as yucca and sweet potato, and native fruits such as guava; from the Spanish came pork, rice, flavor-enhancing spices and different frying techniques; African slave culture brought plantains in their various guises, along with *congrí* (rice and beans cooked together with spices in the same pot); while, from its island neighbors, Cuba shares the unmistakable taste of the Caribbean enshrined in *sofrito*, a base sauce of tomatoes seasoned with onions, peppers, garlic, bay leaf and cumin.

Agropecuarios

Havana has a number of produce markets, called *agropecuarios,* where locals go to buy the ingredients for their dinner. They are interesting places to see the confusing dual economy in full swing.

☑ **Top Tips**

▶ The Coppelia, a 50-year-old ice-cream parlor in a Vedado park, has long been a Havana gossip corner thanks primarily to the omnipresent queues and the table-sharing ethos. If you want to strike up a conversation with a Cuban in Havana, start here.

Havana Restaurants

Lamparilla 361 Tapas & Cervezas Cool, sharp, unpretentious new place where the ambience and service match the excellent food. (p39)

El Rum Rum de la Habana Spanish-influenced fish-focused

restaurant run by a cigar sommelier. (p39)

Doña Eutimia Possibly the best home-style Cuban food in Cuba. (p39)

La Fontana A master of multiple food and style genres, most notably the charcoal grill. (p91)

Café Laurent Refined dining in an otherwise unrefined apartment block in Vedado. (p77)

Starbien Excellent international cuisine at thoroughly reasonable prices served in an attractive Vedado residence. (p77)

Traditional Cuban Restaurants

Doña Eutimia Simply delicious Cuban food just like your abuela (grandma) used to make. (p39)

Donde Lis Traditional Cuban food with a few deft modern twists. (p41)

El Idilio Meat and fish served straight off the grill with lashings of rice and beans. (p79)

Breakfasts

Café del Ángel Fumero Jacqueline The best alfresco nook to start the day, with waffles and strong coffee. (p42)

La Vitrola This late-night joint still manages to open up early for hearty breakfasts. (p42)

La Chucheria Large, economical breakfasts served quickly with Havana's best fruit smoothies on the side. (p79)

El Biky Grab a booth and help yourself to something from its affiliated bakery, Havana's best. (p79)

State-Run Restaurants

Restaurante el Templete This old-town fish specialist is one of the few state-run restaurants that can compete with the private joints. (p42)

El Aljibe Raising its game for the diplomatic crowd with legendary chicken in orange sauce. (p94)

La Torre French-flecked dining with a view atop the Focsa building. (p79)

Italian

Trattoria 5esquinas Blink and you're in Rome, with wafer-thin pizzas and rich seafood pasta dishes. (p40)

La Corte del Príncipe Possibly the most Italian of Havana's Italian restaurants. (p95)

Il Piccolo Hidden at the east end of Playas del Este lies what some claim to be Cuba's finest purveyor of pizza. (p103)

International Cuisine

Nazdarovie Russian food in retro Soviet-era surroundings on the Malecón. (p61)

Casa Miglis This Swedish place in Centro Habana is renowned for its meatballs and toast *skagen*. (p61)

Club Su Miramar Cuba's first Korean restaurant is now open for business in Miramar. (p96)

Best
Historic Sites

Studded with architectural jewels from every era, Havana offers visitors one of the finest collections of historic edifices in the Americas. At a conservative estimate, the Old Town alone contains over 900 buildings of historical importance, with myriad examples of illustrious architecture ranging from intricate baroque to glitzy art deco.

NESTOR NOCI/SHUTTERSTOCK ©

Historic Habana Vieja

Arguably one of the greatest achievements in Cuba in the last 50 years has been the piecing back together of Habana Vieja. This detailed, meticulous, lovingly curated restoration process overseen by Havana's City Historian, Eusebio Leal Spengler, has created one of the historical wonders of the Americas, a kind of Latin American 'Rome' where the past can be peeled off in layers.

Parque Histórico Militar Morro-Cabaña
A two-fort complex and Unesco World Heritage Site that's like a mini-city armed to the hilt. (p26)

Castillo de la Real Fuerza Havana's oldest fort reflects on its history in a seafaring museum packed with scale models of grand

old galleons. (p36; pictured above)

Ermita de Potosí Cuba's oldest church has a simplistic form of beauty. (p111)

Iglesia de Nuestra Señora de Regla The birthplace of one of Cuba's oldest and most fervent religious cults. (p108)

☑ **Top Tips**

► Take time to look inside some of Habana Vieja's historic hotels. Many have beautiful patios and courtyards, all have fine architectural details, and some have attractive bars and restaurants where you can soak up the colonial atmosphere and linger a while longer.

Museo de la Ciudad The history of Havana laid out in one of its finest baroque buildings. (p36)

Best
For Free

Go local in Havana and prices quickly nose-dive. The ferry across the harbor costs practically nothing, metro buses ask for small change, casas particulares charge a 10th of four-star hotel prices (and the service is usually better), and there are plenty of free things to do, if you know where to look.

ANNE-MARIE PALMER/ALAMY ©

Catedral de la Habana Wrapped in a baroque square, the cathedral is Cuba's most visually arresting and unique church. (p30)

Fusterlandia José Fuster's dynamic creativity offers up a dazzling array of street art and costs *nada*. (p88; pictured right)

Hotel Nacional A national monument haunted by the ghosts of famous guests past with free daily tours at 10am. (p74)

Callejón de Hamel Free live rumba music on Sun-days in the melting pot of Havana's Afro-Cuban community. (p55)

Calle Mercaderes This cobbled time-capsule in Habana Vieja is flanked by small, esoteric muse-ums; most are free. (p33)

Ojo del Ciclón Avant-garde art studio and workshop stuffed with wonderfully weird inter-active exhibits. (p36)

Universidad de la Habana Where cash-strapped Cuban students converse in attractive thought-provoking sur-roundings; join them. (p74)

☑ Top Tips

▶ Parque Lenin, in Arroyo Naranjo municipality, 20km south of central Havana, is the city's largest recreational area. The 670 hec-tares of green park-land and beautiful old trees surround an artificial lake. Most of the park's attractions, including rowing, public art and horse-riding, are open 9am to 5pm Tuesday to Sunday, and admission to the park itself is free.

Best
Art & Architecture

Cast an eye over Havana's eclectic architecture and you're halfway to understanding the city's 500-year-old history. The art – showcased in museums, studios, workshops and inspired street-art projects – is equally illuminating. Indeed, Havana is, arguably, one of the most exciting emerging art cities in the Americas.

STEFANIE METZGER/SHUTTERSTOCK ©

Architectural Styles

Havana's classic and most prevalent architectural styles are baroque and neoclassicism. Baroque designers began sharpening their quills in the 1750s; neoclassicism gained the ascendancy in the 1820s and continued, amid numerous revivals, until the 1920s. Trademark buildings of the American era (1902–59) exhibited art deco and, later on, modernist styles. Art nouveau played a cameo role during this period influenced by Catalan *modernisme*; recognizable art nouveau curves and embellishments can be seen on pivotal east–west axis streets in Centro Habana. Ostentatious eclecticism, courtesy of the Americans, characterized Havana's rich and growing suburbs from the 1910s onwards.

Havana's Art

Havana isn't traditionally cited in the pantheon of great art cities alongside New York, Paris, Florence or Barcelona, but, arguably, it should be. An unconventional mix of Spanish classicism, European avant-gardism, native primitivism and American modernism, which has developed for several centuries in its own tropical setting, has endowed the Cuban capital with a unique and refreshingly independent art culture.

Art

Fusterlandia A whole neighborhood covered in a giddy array of mosaics, tiles and lurid paintings. (p88)

Fábrica de Arte Cubano Probing, cutting-edge, always surprising art unleashed in this unique art 'factory.' (p83)

Museo Nacional de Bellas Artes The whole history of Cuban art supported by a commendable collection of international masterpieces. (p50)

Callejón de Hamel Cradle of Havana's Afro-Cuban culture and colorful exponent of street art. (p55)

Centro de Arte Contemporáneo Wifredo Lam The best art on the contemporary scene is displayed in this colonial house named for Cuba's finest artist. (p38)

Architecture

Catedral de la Habana This curvaceous stone colossus is the pinnacle of Cuban baroque. (p30)

Plaza Vieja Havana's most multifarious square exhibits every architectural style from mudéjar to art nouveau. (p28)

Capitolio Nacional A towering example of 20th-century neoclassicism and a close copy of the US Capitol building. (p58; pictured left)

Edificio Bacardí One of the finest examples of art deco architecture in the Americas. (p36)

Hotel Nacional This turreted hotel is one of Havana's most emblematic buildings both inside and out. (p74)

Cafes Doubling up as Art Galleries

Café Madrigal Weird, wacky and Warhol-esque fount of good cocktails and even better art. (p80)

El Dandy Photo art brightens up your breakfast cuppa in this quirky Habana Vieja cafe. (p42)

Espacios Huge canvases offer talking points for cocktail-quaffing artists. (p91)

Café Mamainé Cool, mainly local spot where the walls are hung with

Vedado's latest creative offerings. (p80)

Churches

Catedral de la Habana The pinnacle of baroque architecture in Cuba. (p30)

Iglesia y Convento de Nuestra Señora de la Merced Havana's finest church interior is a riot of frescoes and gilded trimmings. (p37)

Iglesia Jesús de Miramar Worth a visit for both its architecture and art, especially its colorful stations of the cross. (p91)

Convento & Iglesia del Carmen Understated gem of a church in Centro Habana with beautifully tiled interior. (p60)

Iglesia de Nuestra Señora del Rosario

This **church** (Calle 24, btwn 31 & 33, Santa María del Rosario; ☺8am-6pm Tue-Sun), in the Outer Havana suburb of Santa María del Rosario, was built in 1760 in classic baroque style. It's known for its gleaming gold interior made up of a gilded mahogany altar and some equally sumptuous side altars fashioned in the churrigueresque style.

Best
For Kids

Cubans love kids and kids invariably love Cuba. Welcome to a culture where children still play freely in the street. There's something wonderfully old-fashioned about kids' entertainment here, which is less about computer games and more about messing around in the plaza with an improvised baseball bat and a rolled-up ball of plastic.

Planetario (📞7-864-9544; Mercaderes No 311, Plaza Vieja; CUC$10; 🕐10am-3pm Wed-Sun) Havana's planetarium includes a scale reproduction of the solar system inside a giant orb, a simulation of the Big Bang, and a theater that allows viewing of over 6000 stars. All pretty exciting stuff. It's only accessible by guided tours booked in advance. Tours take place Wednesday to Sunday and can be booked (in person) on Monday and Tuesday.

Circo Trompoloco (Map p92, A1; www.circonacional decuba.cu; cnr Av 5 & Calle 112, Playa; CUC$5-10; 🕐7pm Fri, 4pm & 7pm Sat & Sun; 👫) Havana's

permanent 'Big Top', with a weekend matinee, features strongmen, contortionists and acrobats.

Isla del Coco (Map p92, A2; Av 5 & Calle 112, Playa; CUC$5; 🕐noon-8pm Fri-Sun) A huge Chinese-built amusement park in western Playa with big wheels, bumper cars, roller coasters, the works.

Parque Maestranza (Av Carlos Manuel de Céspedes; CUC$3; 🕐10am-5pm) A small-scale but fun kids playground (for children from four to 12 years) with inflatable castles and other games overlooking the harbor.

Maqueta de la Habana Vieja (Mercaderes No 114;

☑ **Top Tips**

▶ Playas del Este (pictured above) offers a vast expanse of sandy beaches 20km east of Havana, with plenty of water toys available to rent. It makes a good day trip for families with kids.

CUC$1.50; 🕐9am-6:30pm; 👫) Herein lies a 1:500 scale model of Habana Vieja complete with an authentic soundtrack meant to replicate a day in the life of the city. It's incredibly detailed and provides an excellent way of geographically acquainting yourself with the city's historical core.

Best
Tours & Activities

Aside from Spanish-language courses, Havana offers a large number of learning activities for aspiring students. Dancing and art classes are the most popular. On terra firma, outdoor recreational activities include horseback riding and cycling. In the water, diving and kite-boarding prevail. Havana has a large menu of organized tours, with private operators now supplementing the standard diet of government-run day-trips.

BERTRAND GARDEL/SHUTTERSTOCK ©

☑ Top Tips

▶ Havana's two marinas, Marina Tarará (east) and Marina Hemingway (west), lie in its outer suburbs. Both offer numerous fishing, diving and boating opportunities. It's best to book these activities in advance at the tour desk of any Havana hotel of three stars and above.

Tour Agencies

State-run tourist agencies, such as Gaviota, Cubanacán and Cubatur generally offer a similar diet of tours including a general city tour (CUC$19) and a Hemingway tour (CUC$20).

San Cristóbal Agencia de Viajes, the agency run by the City Historian, does a few more interesting specialist tours focusing on topics such as religion, art and architecture.

Several private tour operators have taken off in recent years, with quirky little excursions such as a Havana 'Mob tour' or a guided city bicycle tour.

Tours & Activities

La Casa del Son Learn to dance like a Cuban at this dance school in Habana Vieja. (p37; pictured above)

CubaRuta Bikes Discover the monuments and secrets of Havana on a brilliant bike tour. (p74)

Havana Super Tour Join up for a 'Mob tour' or an art deco architectural tour in a classic American car. (p61)

Havana Kiteboarding Club Rent a board or book a lesson to try Cuba's newest sport at beachside Tarará. (p103)

Best
Gay & Lesbian

In its early days, the revolution had a hostile attitude toward homosexuality. But since the 1990s the tide has been turning, spearheaded somewhat ironically by Mariela Castro, daughter of current president, Raúl Castro, and the director of the Cuban National Center for Sex Education in Havana.

VWPICS/ALAMY S ©

Beaches, Film Nights & Festivals

In more discriminatory days, Havana's only gay beach was Mi Cayito, a quiet secluded stretch of Playa Boca Ciega in Playas del Este. The beach remains popular. You can now also enjoy gay film nights at the Icaic headquarters on the corner of Calles 23 and 12 in Vedado and, since 2009, an annual gay parade along Calle 23 in mid-May. Legally, lesbians enjoy the same rights as gay men, though there is a less evident lesbian 'scene.'

LGBT Locales

Cabaret Las Vegas Edgy local cabaret well-known for its drag shows. (p81)

Café Cantante Mi Habana Rambunctious club in Cuba's National Theater complex with a Saturday night drag show. (p71)

Toke Infanta y 25 Gay-friendly café in the western reaches of Vedado that sells cheap snacks. (p80)

Coppelia Made famous by the film *Fresa y Chocolate,* this ice-cream parlor and its surrounding park are popular with Havana's LGBT crowd. (p70)

Malecón A favorite meeting point for Havana's gay life. (p55)

Café Fresa y Chocolate Bar attached to Cuba's film institute that holds occasional gay film nights. (p71)

☑ Top Tips

▶ Called the world's 'longest sofa' for good reason, Havana's 7km-long Malecón sea drive is the best place to find out who's who and what's what in the city. Each area has a different flavor. The section close to the intersection with La Rampa (Calle 23) is a popular gay meeting point.

Best
Festivals & Events

Havana has a packed program of annual events. There's a summer Carnaval, multiple music festivals (including the much lauded December Festival Internacional de Jazz), sports events such as the Marabana (marathon), and big international occasions that pull in famous names from abroad.

Feria Internacional del Libro (www.filcuba.cult.cu; ☙Feb) First held in 1930, the International Book Fair is headquartered at Havana's Fortaleza de San Carlos de la Cabaña, but it later goes on the road to other cities. Highlights include book presentations, special readings and the prestigious Casa de las Américas prize.

Carnaval de la Habana Parades, dancing, music, colorful costumes and striking effigies – Havana's annual summer shindig might not be as famous as its more rootsy Santiago de Cuba counterpart, but the celebrations and processions along the Malecón leave plenty of other city carnivals in the shade.

Festival Internacional de Ballet de la Habana (www.festivalballethabana.cu; ☙Oct) Cuba demonstrates its ballet prowess at this annual festival, with energetic leaps and graceful pirouettes starting in late October.

Marabana (www.havanamarathon.net; ☙Nov) The popular Havana marathon (pictured above) draws between 2000 and 3000 competitors from around the globe. It's a two-lap course, though there is also a half-marathon and 5km and 10km races.

Festival Internacional del Nuevo Cine Latinoamericano (www.habanafilmfestival.com; ☙Dec) Widely lauded celebration of Cuba's massive film culture, with plenty of nods to other Latin American countries. The festival is held at various cinemas and theaters across the city.

Festival Internacional de Jazz (http://jazzcuba.com) The cream of Cuban music festivals arrives every December like a Christmas present. In the past it has attracted the greats, Dizzy Gillespie and Max Roach among them, along with a perfect storm of Cuban talent.

Best
Shopping

Sixty years of *socialismo* didn't do much for Havana's shopping scene. That said, there are some decent outlets for travelers and tourists, particularly for those after the standard Cuban shopping triumvirate of rum, cigars and coffee. Art is another lucrative field. Havana's art scene is cutting edge and ever changing, and browsers will find many galleries in which to while away hours.

KARI548/SHUTTERSTOCK ©

☑ **Top Tips**

▶ Calle Obispo, Habana Vieja's main drag, is peppered with artists' studios and painters at their easels. This is one of the best places to buy art directly from the artist.

Places to Shop

Centro Cultural Antiguos Almacenes de Deposito San José Havana's largest and most revealing private enterprise market. (p47)

Memorias Librería Find antique collectibles in this jewel of an old book and magazine shop. (p65)

Clandestina Recycled clothes are the shape of things to come in this new privately run Havana boutique. (p47)

La Casa del Habano Quinta Where the cigar glitterati go to buy their smokes. (p97)

Cigar shops

Casa del Habano – Hostal Conde de Villanueva Smoke shop in a historic Havana hotel known for its expert staff and rollers. (p47)

Real Fábrica de Tabacos Partagás – Shop The factory's moved, but the shop is still open in a building behind the Capitolio Nacional. (p65)

Bookshops

Memorias Librería Antique bookshop with a sideline in vintage magazines and other small collectibles. (p65)

Librería Venecia Rare poster art, dog-eared books and the odd hidden treasure waiting to be found. (p47)

Plaza de Armas Secondhand Book Market A visit to the famous alfresco market in Plaza de Armas is a Havana rite of passage. (p47; pictured above)

Survival Guide

Survival Guide

Before You Go

When to Go

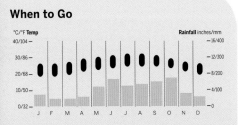

°C/°F **Temp**
40/104 —
30/86 —
20/68 —
10/50 —
0/32 —

J F M A M J J A S O N D

Rainfall inches/mm
— 16/400
— 12/300
— 8/200
— 4/100
— 0

➡ **Feb** February is peak season, meaning there's extra life in the city and plenty of extra-curricular activities, including a cigar festival and an international book fair.

➡ **Aug-Oct** August is hot, but fun, especially if you time your visit to coincide with Havana's ostentatious Carnaval.

If you want to avoid the stifling heat, come in October, a quiet month when there's still plenty to do.

➡ **Dec** Busier (for a reason) is December, when people line up for the Festival Internacional del Nuevo Cine Latinoamericano, Cuba's premiere movie shindig.

Book Your Stay

With literally thousands of casas particulares (private houses) letting out rooms, you'll never struggle to find accommodation in Havana. Rock-bottom budget hotels can match casas for price, but not comfort. There's a dearth of decent hotels in the midrange price bracket, while Havana's top-end hotels are plentiful and offer oodles of atmosphere, even if the overall standards can't always match facilities elsewhere in the Caribbean.

Useful Websites

➡ **Cuba Casas** (www.cubacasas.net) Canadian-based website in English and French with hundreds of regularly updated casas particulares listings and photos.

➡ **Casa Particular Organization** (www.casaparticularcuba.org) Comprehensive listings of Cuba's private homestays.

➡ **A Nash Travel** (www.nashtravel.com) Long-standing Canada-based travel agency that can book any hotel in the city.

➡ **Lonely Planet** (lonely planet.com/cuba/hotels) Recommendations and bookings.

Best Budget

Hostal Peregrino Consulado (www.hostalperegrino.com) Friendly and charming cross between a decent hotel and a backpackers hostel.

Central Yard Inn (centralyardinn@gmail.com) Wonderfully restored private house in the middle of Vedado's main hotel district.

Greenhouse (fabio.quintana@infomed.sld.cu) Beautifully decorated period house with multiple rooms in the heart of Habana Vieja.

Casa 1932 (www.casahabana.net) A private rental dedicated to the age of art deco.

Best Midrange

Casavana Cuba (www.casavanacuba.com) The king of Havana's casas particulares is a bit pricier, but worth it.

Conde de Ricla Hostal (www.condedericlahostal.com) Small private hotel in Plaza Vieja with a boutique sheen.

Villa Teresa (marlene7667@yahoo.es) Plush new private rental in Miramar with lily-white rooms.

Best Top End

Hotel Saratoga (www.saratogahotel-cuba.com) Top-notch service meets historical ambience in one of Havana's best restoration jobs.

Hotel Iberostar Parque Central (www.iberostar.com) Multiple facilities and sharp service at this centrally located five-star.

Hotel Meliá Cohiba (www.meliacuba.com) The best business hotel in Havana stands tall on a prime location on the Malecón sea drive.

Hotel Meliá Habana (www.meliacuba.com) The best hotel in Miramar has Cuba's largest swimming pool and large business-friendly rooms.

Arriving in Havana

José Martí International Airport

➡ **Aeropuerto Internacional José Martí** (www.havana-airport.org; Av Rancho Boyeros) is at Rancho Boyeros, 25km southwest of Havana via Av de la Independencia. There are four terminals.

➡ Public transportation from the airport into central Havana is practically nonexistent. A standard taxi will cost you approximately CUC$20 to CUC$25 (30 to 40 minutes).

Víazul Bus Terminal

➡ **Víazul** (📞 7-881-5652, 7-881-1413; www.viazul.com; Calle 26, cnr Zoológica, Nuevo Vedado; ⏱ 7am-9:30pm) covers most destinations of interest to travelers, in safe, air-conditioned coaches.

➡ You board all Víazul buses at their inconveniently located terminal 3km southwest of Plaza de la Revolución. This is

Documents Required on Entry

➡ Passport valid for at least one month beyond your departure date

➡ Cuba 'tourist card' filled out correctly

➡ Proof of travel medical insurance (random checks at airport)

➡ Evidence of sufficient funds for the duration of your stay

➡ Return air ticket

where you'll also have to come to buy tickets from the Venta de Boletines office.

➡ Buses get busy particularly in peak season (November through March), so it's wise to book up to a week in advance. You can also book online. Full bus schedules are available on the website.

La Coubre Train Station

➡ Trains to most parts of Cuba depart from **La Coubre station** (Túnel de la Habana), while the Estación Central de Ferrocarriles is being refurbished until 2018 or later. La Coubre is on the southwestern side of Habana Vieja.

➡ At the time of research, Cuba's main train (No 11), the *Tren Francés* (still using its increasingly dilapidated French SNCF carriages), was running every fourth day between Havana and Santiago, stopping in Santa Clara and Camagüey.

➡ Services are routinely delayed or canceled. Always double-check scheduling and which terminal your train will leave from.

Terminal Sierra Maestra

➡ Cruise ships dock at the **Terminal Sierra Maestra** (Cruise Terminal; Map p34), adjacent to Plaza de San Francisco de Asís on the cusp of Habana Vieja.

Getting Around

Bus

➡ The handy hop-on/hop-off **Habana Bus Tour** runs on two routes, numbers T1 and T3. The main stop is in Parque Central opposite the Hotel Inglaterra. This is the pick-up point for bus T1, which runs from Habana Vieja via Centro Habana, the Malecón, Calle 23 and Plaza de la Revolución to La Cecilia at the west end of Playa; and bus T3, which runs from Centro Habana to Playas del Este (via Parque Histórico Militar Morro-Cabaña). All-day tickets for T1/T3 are CUC$10/5. Services run from 9am to 7pm and routes and stops are clearly marked on all bus stops.

➡ Havana's metro bus service calls on a relatively modern fleet of Chinese-made 'bendy' buses and is far less dilapidated than it used to be. These buses run regularly along 17 different routes, connecting most parts of the city with the suburbs. Fares are 40 centavos (five centavos if you're using convertibles). Cuban buses are crowded and little used by tourists.

Guard your valuables closely.

Taxi

➡ The most common taxis are the yellow cabs of **Cubataxi** (🕿 7-796-6666; Calle 478, btwn Av 7 & 7B). Other taxis might be Ladas, old American cars or modern Toyotas.

➡ Always agree on a fare before you get in. The cheapest official cabs charge around CUC$1 as the starting fare, then CUC$0.50 per kilometer.

➡ Since 2011 legal private taxis have become more common, though they're often older yellow-and-black Ladas. You've got more chance haggling here.

➡ Shared Cuban taxis (usually old American cars) charge in *moneda nacional* and run on several well-established routes in Havana.

➡ The small yellow egg-shaped 'Coco taxis' are a well known tourist rip-off.

Boat

➡ Passenger ferries shuttle across the harbor to Regla and Casablanca, leaving every 15 or 20 minutes from the recently refurbished terminal **Emboque de Luz** (Map p34, D6), at the corner of San Pedro and Santa Clara, on the southeast side of Habana Vieja. The fare is a flat 10 centavos.

Essential Information

Business Hours

Banks 9am–3pm Monday to Friday

Cadeca Money Exchanges 9am–7pm Monday to Saturday and 9am–noon Sunday. Many top-end city hotels offer money exchange late into the evening.

Pharmacies 8am–8pm

Post Offices 8am–5pm Monday to Saturday, sometimes longer

Restaurants Noon–midnight

Shops 9am–5pm Monday to Saturday and 9am–noon Sunday

Internet Access

➡ Cuba's internet service provider is national phone company **Etecsa**. Etecsa

People-to-People Tours for US Travelers

Since January 2011, Americans have been able to travel legally to Cuba on government sanctioned people-to-people trips (cultural trips with licensed providers). While self-directed, individual travel was permitted by the Obama administration for educational purposes, under the Trump administration's stricter policy toward US-Cuba relations, Americans will be limited to group travel through licensed tour operators.

On these trips, authorized agents handle the license paperwork, leaving participants with fewer legal worries and more downtime to enjoy organized excursions in a similar way to other vacationers. The US Treasury department (www.treasury.gov/resource-center/sanctions/Programs/pages/cuba.aspx) has issued licenses to hundreds of registered people-to-people travel companies since 2011.

Dos and Don'ts

➡ Do stay in casas particulares (private homestays).

➡ Do carry toilet paper and antiseptic hand-wash

➡ Don't drink the tap water.

➡ Do avoid driving in Havana. The city has various public transportation options and reasonably priced taxis. Most neighborhoods are walkable.

➡ Do bring a warm sweater (jumper) for buses – the air-conditioning is often freezing.

➡ Don't rely on US-linked credit or debit cards – despite diplomatic talk, their use in Cuba still hasn't been activated.

➡ Do make advance bookings for accommodations and transportation, especially in peak season.

110V/220V/60Hz

runs various *telepuntos* (internet-cafes-cum-call-centers) in Habana: the main ones are in **Centro Habana** (Águila No 565, cnr Dragones; ⊘8:30am-7pm) and **Habana Vieja** (Habana No 406, cnr Obispo; ⊘9am-7pm).

➡ The drill is to buy a one-hour user card (CUC$1.50) with a scratch-off user code and *contraseña* (password), and either help yourself to a free computer or use it on your own device in one of the city's 30-plus wi-fi hot spots.

➡ Most Havana hotels that are rated three stars and up also have wi-fi. You don't generally have to be a guest to use it.

➡ Popular wi-fi hot spots in Havana include La Rampa (Calle 23 between L and Malecón) in Vedado, the corner of Av de Italia and San Rafael in Centro Habana, and the Miramar Trade Center in Playa.

Electricity

The electrical current in Cuba is 110V with 220V in many tourist hotels and resorts.

110V/220V/60Hz

Money

ATMs

➡ ATMs are now widespread in Havana and usually function pretty efficiently. Check with your home bank before your departure regarding your own card's functionality in Cuba. Cuban ATMs generally accept non-US-linked Visa credit and debit cards.

➡ Cuban ATMs are notorious for giving out small denomination notes. You might find yourself trying to stuff CUC$200 worth of CUC$3 notes into your pocket.

Credit Cards

Cuba is primarily a cash economy. Credit cards are accepted in resort hotels and some city hotels. The acceptance of credit cards has become more widespread in Cuba in recent years and was aided by the legalization of US and US-linked credit and debit cards in early 2015.

However, change is still a work in process, and US residents should note that at the time of research, debit and credit cards from the USA could still not be used. While services can still be booked with credit cards from the US on the internet, in country it's another story. Residents of the US can wire money via Western Union, though this requires help from a third party and hefty fees.

When weighing up whether to use a credit card or cash, bear in mind that the charges levied by Cuban banks are similar for both (around 3%). However, your home bank may charge additional fees for ATM and credit-card transactions. An increasing number of debit cards work in Cuba, but it's best to check with both your home bank and the local Cuban bank before using them.

Ideally, you should arrive in Cuba with a stash of cash, and a credit and debit card as back-up.

Almost all private business in Cuba (ie with casas particulares and paladares) is still conducted in cash.

Public Holidays

Officially Cuba (and hence Havana) has nine public holidays.

January 1 Triunfo de la Revolución (Liberation Day)

January 2 Día de la Victoria (Victory of the Armed Forces)

May 1 Día de los Trabajadores (International Worker's Day)

July 25 Commemoration of Moncada Attack

July 26 Día de la Rebeldía Nacional – Commemoration of Moncada Attack

July 27 Commemoration of Moncada Attack

October 10 Día de la Indepedencia (Independence Day)

December 25 Navidad (Christmas Day)

December 31 New Year's Eve

Safe Travel

➡ Havana is not a dangerous city, especially when compared to other metropolitan areas in North and South America; however, petty crime against tourists in Havana is a possibility.

➡ Bring a money belt and keep it on you at all times.

➡ In hotels use a safety deposit box (if there is one) and never leave money, passports or credit cards lying around during the day.

➡ In bars and restaurants it is wise to check your change.

➡ Agree on taxi fares before getting into a cab.

➡ Don't change money on the street.

➡ If you've prebooked a casa particular, or are using Lonely Planet to find one, make sure you turn up without a commission-seeking *jinetero* (hustler).

Toilets

Havana isn't over-endowed with clean and accessible public toilets. Most tourists slip into upscale hotels if they're caught short. Even there, restrooms often lack toilet paper, soap and door locks. Make sure you tip the ladyman at the door.

Tourist Information

State-run Infotur books tours and has maps, phonecards and useful free brochures.

Pretty much every hotel in Havana has some type of state-run tourist information desk.

Infotur offices in Havana:

Airport (☎7-642-6101; Terminal 3, Aeropuerto Internacional José Martí; ⏰24hr)

Habana del Este (Av de las Terrazas, Edificio los Corales, btwn Calles 10 & 11; ⏰8:15am-4:15pm)

Habana Vieja (Map p34; ☎7-863-6884; cnr Obispo & San Ignacio; ⏰9:30am-noon & 12:30-5pm)

Habana Vieja (Map p34; ☎7-866-4153; Obispo No 524, btwn Bernaza & Villegas; ⏰9:30am-5:30pm)

Playa (cnr Av 5 & Calle 112, Playa; ⏰8:30am-noon & 12:30-5pm Mon-Sat)

Licenses for US Visitors

➡ The US government issues two sorts of licenses for travel to Cuba: 'specific' and 'general.' Specific licenses require a lengthy and sometimes complicated application process and are considered on a case-by-case basis; their application should start at least 45 days before your intended date of departure.

➡ Most visitors will travel under general licenses. General licenses are self-qualifying and don't require travelers to notify the Office of Foreign Assets Control (OFAC) of their travel plans. Travelers sign an affidavit stating the purpose of travel and purchase a Cuban Visa at check-in when departing the United States via flights. Visas average $50, purchased through airlines or established third parties. Note that the Trump administration has eliminated individual travel under the 'educational purpose' license category.

➡ You might need supporting documentation to back up your claim when you book your flight ticket. Check with the **US Department of the Treasury** (www.treasury.gov/resource-center/sanctions/Programs/pages/cuba.aspx) to see if you qualify for a license.

Travellers with Disabilities

Cuba's inclusive culture extends to disabled travelers, and while facilities may be lacking, the generous nature of Cubans generally compensates. Sight-impaired travelers will be helped across streets and given priority in lines. The same holds true for travelers in wheelchairs, although they'll find the few ramps ridiculously steep and will have trouble in colonial parts of town where sidewalks are narrow and streets are cobblestone. Elevators are often out of order. Etecsa phone centers have telephone equipment for the hearing-impaired, and TV programs are broadcast with closed captioning.

Download Lonely Planet's free Accessible Travel guide from http://lptravel.to/Accessible-Travel.

Visas

➡ Regular tourists who plan to spend up to two months in Cuba do not need visas. Instead, you get a *tarjeta de turista* (tourist card), which is valid for 30 days and can be extended once you're in Cuba (Canadians get 90 days plus the option of a 90-day extension).

➡ Package tourists receive their card with their other travel documents. Those going 'air only' usually buy the tourist card from the travel agency or airline office that sells them the plane ticket, but policies vary (eg Canadian airlines give out tourist cards on their airplanes), so you'll need to check ahead with the airline office via phone or email.

➡ In some cases, you may be required to buy and/or pick up the card at your departure airport, sometimes at the flight gate itself some minutes before departure.

➡ Once in Havana, tourist-card extensions or replacements cost another CUC$25. You cannot leave Cuba without presenting your tourist card.

➡ You are not permitted entry to Cuba without an onward ticket.

Language

Spanish pronunciation is pretty straightforward – Spanish spelling is phonetically consistent, meaning that there's a clear and consistent relationship between what you see in writing and how it's pronounced. Also, most Latin American Spanish sounds are pronounced the same as their English counterparts. Note though that the **kh** in our pronunciation guides is a throaty sound (like the 'ch' in the Scottish loch), **v** and **b** are similar to the English 'b' (but softer, between a 'v' and a 'b'), and **r** is strongly rolled. If you read our colored pronunciation guides as if they were English, you'll be understood just fine. The stressed syllables are in italics.

To enhance your trip with a phrasebook, visit **lonelyplanet.com**. Lonely Planet iPhone phrasebooks are available through the Apple App store.

Basics

Hello. *Hola.* o·la

Goodbye. *Adiós.* a·dyos

Sorry. *Lo siento.* lo syen·to

Yes./No. *Sí./No.* see/no

Please. *Por favor.* por fa·vor

How are you?
¿Qué tal? ke tal

Fine, thanks.
Bien, gracias. byen gra·syas

Excuse me.
Perdón. per·don

Thank you.
Gracias. gra·syas

You're welcome.
De nada. de na·da

My name is ...
Me llamo ... me ya·mo ...

What's your name?
¿Cómo se ko·mo se
llama usted? ya·ma oo·ste (pol)

Do you speak English?
¿Habla inglés? a·bla een·gles (pol)

I don't understand.
Yo no entiendo. yo no en·tyen·do

Eating & Drinking

What would you recommend?
¿Qué recomienda? ke re·ko·myen·da

I don't eat ...
No como ... no ko·mo ...

That was delicious!
¡Estaba es·ta·ba
buenísimo! bwe·nee·see·mo

Please bring the bill.
Por favor nos trae por fa·vor nos tra·e
la cuenta. la kwen·ta

Cheers!
¡Salud! sa·loo

I'd like to book a table for ...
Quisiera reservar kee·sye·ra re·ser·var
una mesa para ... oo·na me·sa pa·ra ...

   (eight) o'clock
   las (ocho) las (o·cho)

   (two) people
   (dos) personas (dos) per·so·nas

Shopping

How much is it?
¿Cuánto cuesta? kwan·to kwes·ta

I'd like to buy ...
Quisiera kee·*sye*·ra
comprar... kom·*prar* ...

I'm just looking.
Sólo estoy so·lo es·*toy*
mirando. mee·*ran*·do

May I look at it?
¿Puedo verlo? *pwe*·do *ver*·lo

I don't like it.
No me gusta. no me *goos*·ta

That's too expensive.
Es muy caro. es mooy *ka*·ro

Can you lower the price?
¿Podría bajar po·*dree*·a ba·*khar*
un poco el precio? oon po·ko el *pre*·syo

Emergencies

Help! *¡Socorro!* so·*ko*·ro

Go away! *¡Vete!* *ve*·te

Call ...! *¡Llame a ...!* *ya*·me a ...

 a doctor
 un médico oon *me*·dee·ko

 the police
 la policía la po·lee·*see*·a

I'm lost. (m/f)
Estoy perdido/a. es·toy per·*dee*·do/a

I'm ill.
Estoy enfermo/a. es·toy en·*fer*·mo/a

Where are the toilets?
¿Dónde están *don*·de es·*tan*
los servicios? los ser·*vee*·syos

Time & Numbers

morning	*mañana*	ma·*nya*·na
afternoon	*tarde*	*tar*·de
evening	*noche*	*no*·che
yesterday	*ayer*	a·*yer*
today	*hoy*	oy
tomorrow	*mañana*	ma·*nya*·na
1	*uno*	*oo*·no
2	*dos*	dos
3	*tres*	tres
4	*cuatro*	*kwa*·tro
5	*cinco*	*seen*·ko
6	*seis*	seys
7	*siete*	*sye*·te
8	*ocho*	*o*·cho
9	*nueve*	*nwe*·ve
10	*diez*	dyes

What time is it?
¿Qué hora es? ke *o*·ra es

It's (10) o'clock.
Son (las diez). son (las dyes)

It's half past (one).
Es (la una) es (la *oo*·na)
y media. ee *me*·dya

Transport & Directions

Where's ...?
¿Dónde está ...? *don*·de es·*ta* ...

What's the address?
¿Cuál es kwal es
la dirección? la dee·rek·*syon*

I want to go to ...
Quisiera ir a ... kee·*sye*·ra eer a ...

Does it stop at ...?
¿Para en ...? *pa*·ra en ...

What stop is this?
¿Cuál es esta kwal es *es*·ta
parada? pa·*ra*·da

What time does it arrive/leave?
¿A qué hora a ke *o*·ra
llega/sale? *ye*·ga/*sa*·le

Behind the Scenes

Send Us Your Feedback

We love to hear from travelers – your comments help make our books better. We read every word, and we guarantee that your feedback goes straight to the authors. Visit **lonelyplanet.com/contact** to submit your updates and suggestions.

Note: We may edit, reproduce and incorporate your comments in Lonely Planet products such as guidebooks, websites and digital products, so let us know if you don't want your comments reproduced or your name acknowledged. For a copy of our privacy policy visit lonelyplanet.com/privacy.

Brendan's Thanks

Thanks to all my Cuban amigos, many of whom helped me immensely during this research (and have been doing so for years). Special thanks to Carlos Sarmiento, Luis Miguel, Julio and Elsa Roque, and to my wife, Liz, and son, Kieran, for accompanying me on the road.

Acknowledgements

Cover Photograph: Classic car on Paseo de Martí (El Prado), Susanne Kremer/4Corners ©

Contents photograph: Malecón sea drive, lazyllama/Shutterstock ©

This Book

This 1st edition of Lonely Planet's *Pocket Havana* guidebook was researched and written by Brendan Sainsbury. This guidebook was produced by the following:

Destination Editor Bailey Freeman

Product Editor Grace Dobell

Senior Cartographer Mark Griffiths

Book Designer Clara Monitto

Assisting Editors Nigel Chin, Victoria Harrison, Gabrielle Stefanos

Cover Researcher Naomi Parker

Thanks to Carly Hall, Kate Kiely, Kate Mathews, Carolyn McCarthy, Kirsten Rawlings, Tony Wheeler, Amanda Williamson

Index

See also separate subindexes for:

🍽 Eating p157

🍷 Drinking p158

★ Entertainment p158

🛍 Shopping p158

✕ Eating